EVERYMAN,
I WILL GO WITH THEE
AND BE THY GUIDE,
IN THY MOST NEED
TO GO BY THY SIDE

EVERYMAN'S LIBRARY
POCKET POETS

Poems of
New York

Selected and edited by
Elizabeth Schmidt

EVERYMAN'S LIBRARY

POCKET POETS

Alfred A. Knopf · New York · Toronto

THIS IS A BORZOI BOOK
PUBLISHED BY ALFRED A. KNOPF

This selection by Elizabeth Schmidt first published in
Everyman's Library, 2002
Copyright © 2002 by Everyman's Library

Seventeenth printing

A list of acknowledgments to copyright owners appears at the back
of this volume.

www.randomhouse.com/everymans

ISBN 978-0-375-41504-3

Typography by Peter B. Willberg
Typeset in the UK by AccComputing, North Barrow, Somerset
Printed and bound in Germany by GGP Media GmbH, Pössneck

CONTENTS

11

12

14

FOREWORD

New York as we know it was conceived in 1811, when three commissioners unfurled their eight-foot-long plan for the city's physical organization. The result: a grid of 2,028 more or less equal blocks stretching from The Battery off into the hills of Upper Manhattan. The plan was met with wonder, bewilderment, and outrage. Would the city truly expand past what is now midtown, where Broadway turned from country road to old Indian trail, running through thick woods and grazing pasture? Where were the big avenues? Where were those culs-de-sac and circular streets that London and Paris had? Where were the expanses for grand residences? But these early city planners knew that the crowds that had just started pouring into New York would have to live together on this fairly small island, bound by two rivers, and that small, right-angled buildings were the fastest and cheapest to build.

Walt Whitman was born eight years later, and came of age as city prowler and great lyric poet just as this phenomenon of speculative planning took shape. He marveled as the "numberless crowded streets" and "high growths of iron ... splendidly uprising toward clear skies" emerged and spread. Whitman embraced the splendor and the squalor of the city, recognizing the democratic potential of life lived on all those equal blocks. And his walks from Brooklyn up Broadway at the dawn of the industrial age inspired him not only to modernize but also to *urbanize* poetry.

In a sense, the challenge Whitman faced as he set out to write this new poetry was similar to the challenges city planners and architects have felt since the grid determined the development of Manhattan. Whitman faced the printed page; builders, their square lot. Whitman responded by filling every square inch of the page with poetry. His long catalogues of feelings, impressions, and observations flowed well beyond the borders of most traditional poetry. Whitman invented a poetic form for capturing the richness and contrasts, the simultaneity and density of New York life. His cascading, unconventionally punctuated phrases speed along, or stop suddenly, in ways that still correspond to the sensory experience of New York street life. It was a new language for a new life style, one that paved the way for an astonishing range of voices: from Hart Crane's "swift/unfractioned idiom" and Langston Hughes' "drowsy syncopated tune," to James Schuyler's ode to "mutable, delicate, expendable, ugly, mysterious" tenements and June Jordan's take on "the cool/formalities of Madison Avenue/after midnight."

The poems collected in this anthology have about as much or as little in common as the buildings on an average city block—but they all share a desire to record the fleeting, shifting, "parti-colored" essences of New York life in their own particular form and diction. "We are here now but soon/we will not be here" begins a poem by Malena Mörling, one of the youngest poets in this volume. "Can you sing yourself, your life, your place/on the warm planet earth" asks Amiri Baraka in his portrait of Harlem. For generations New York poets have worked to capture the immediacy of urban experience, even as it is vanishing, like an ex-lover around a corner or the fading reflection of a sunset in a glass curtain wall.

I began collecting the poems in this anthology just after the September 11th attack on the World Trade Center—an attack I witnessed with my family, neighbors and strangers from the stoop of my building in lower Manhattan. A week later, *The New Yorker* magazine published a poem by the Polish poet Adam Zagajewski, written months before the event, that urged readers to "praise the mutilated world/and the gray feather a thrush lost,/and the gentle light that strays and vanishes/and returns." This poem was followed several weeks later by C. K. Williams' three-part meditation "War," which contains these lines:

These things that happen in the particle of time we have to
    be alive,

these violations which almost always more than any altar,
     ark, or mosque
embody sanctity by enacting so precisely sanctity's
     desecration.

For many of us grieving for New York, here in the city
and around the world, these poems became directives
for appreciating all we take for granted. New York con-
tinually reminds us that time passes. New buildings go
up and old ones come down. Hundreds of faces pass us
by on the street each day. Poets who have written about
New York are masters at preserving, and allowing us
to cherish, moments of life in this theater of chance and
change.

ELIZABETH SCHMIDT

MANNAHATTA

I was asking for something specific and perfect for
    my city
Whereupon lo! upsprang the aboriginal name.
Now I see what there is in a name, a word, liquid, sane,
    unruly, musical, self-sufficient,
I see that the word of my city is that word from of old,
Because I see that word nested in nests of water-bays,
    superb,
Rich, hemm'd thick all around with sailships and
    steamships, an island sixteen miles long,
    solid-founded,
Numberless crowded streets, high growths of iron,
    slender, strong, light, splendidly uprising toward
    clear skies,
Tides swift and ample, well-loved by me, toward
    sundown,
The flowing sea-currents, the little islands, larger
    adjoining islands, the heights, the villas,
The countless masts, the white shore-steamers, the
    lighters, the ferry-boats, the black sea-steamers
    well-model'd,
The down-town streets, the jobbers' houses of
    business, the houses of business of the ship-
    merchants and money-brokers, the river-streets,

Immigrants arriving, fifteen or twenty thousand in
      a week,
The carts hauling goods, the manly race of drivers of
      horses, the brown-faced sailors,
The summer air, the bright sun shining, and the sailing
      clouds aloft,
The winter snows, the sleigh-bells, the broken ice in
      the river, passing along up or down with the
      flood-tide or ebb-tide,
The mechanics of the city, the masters, well-form'd,
      beautiful-faced, looking you straight in the eyes,
Trottoirs throng'd, vehicles, Broadway, the women,
      the shops and shows,
A million people—manners free and superb—open
      voices—hospitality—the most courageous and
      friendly young men,
City of hurried and sparkling waters! city of spires
      and masts!
City nested in bays! my city!

BROADWAY

What hurrying human tides, or day or night!
What passions, winnings, losses, ardors, swim
    thy waters!
What whirls of evil, bliss and sorrow, stem thee!
What curious questioning glances—glints of love!
Leer, envy, scorn, contempt, hope, aspiration!
Thou portal—thou arena—thou of the myriad
    long-drawn lines and groups!
(Could but thy flagstones, curbs, façades, tell their
    inimitable tales;
Thy windows rich, and huge hotels—thy side-walks
    wide;)
Thou of the endless sliding, mincing, shuffling feet!
Thou, like the parti-colored world itself—like infinite,
    teeming, mocking life!
Thou visor'd, vast, unspeakable show and lesson!

CROSSING BROOKLYN FERRY

1

Flood-tide below me! I see you face to face!
Clouds of the west—sun there half an hour high—
    I see you also face to face.

Crowds of men and women attired in the usual
    costumes, how curious you are to me!
On the ferry-boats the hundreds and hundreds that
    cross, returning home, are more curious to me
    than you suppose,
And you that shall cross from shore to shore years
    hence are more to me, and more in my
    meditations, than you might suppose.

2

The impalpable sustenance of me from all things at all
    hours of the day,
The simple, compact, well-join'd scheme, myself
    disintegrated, every one disintegrated yet part of
    the scheme,
The similitudes of the past and those of the future,
The glories strung like beads on my smallest sights
    and hearings, on the walk in the street and the
    passage over the river,

The current rushing so swiftly and swimming with me
    far away,
The others that are to follow me, the ties between me
    and them,
The certainty of others, the life, love, sight, hearing of
    others.

Others will enter the gates of the ferry and cross from
    shore to shore,
Others will watch the run of the flood-tide,
Others will see the shipping of Manhattan north and
    west, and the heights of Brooklyn to the south
    and east,
Others will see the islands large and small;
Fifty years hence, others will see them as they cross,
    the sun half an hour high,
A hundred years hence, or ever so many hundred years
    hence, others will see them,
Will enjoy the sunset, the pouring-in of the flood-tide,
    the falling-back to the sea of the ebb-tide.

3

It avails not, time nor place—distance avails not,
I am with you, you men and women of a generation, or
    ever so many generations hence,

Just as you feel when you look on the river and sky,
    so I felt,
Just as any of you is one of a living crowd, I was one
    of a crowd,
Just as you are refresh'd by the gladness of the river
    and the bright flow, I was refresh'd,
Just as you stand and lean on the rail, yet hurry with
    the swift current, I stood yet was hurried,
Just as you look on the numberless masts of ships and
    the thick-stemm'd pipes of steamboats, I look'd.

I too many and many a time cross'd the river of old,
Watched the Twelfth-month sea-gulls, saw them high
    in the air floating with motionless wings,
    oscillating their bodies,
Saw how the glistening yellow lit up parts of their
    bodies and left the rest in strong shadow,
Saw the slow-wheeling circles and the gradual edging
    toward the south,
Saw the reflection of the summer sky in the water,
Had my eyes dazzled by the shimmering track of
    beams,
Look'd at the fine centrifugal spokes of light round the
    shape of my head in the sunlit water,
Look'd on the haze on the hills southward and south-
    westward,
Look'd on the vapor as it flew in fleeces tinged with violet,

Look'd toward the lower bay to notice the vessels
  arriving,
Saw their approach, saw aboard those that were near me,
Saw the white sails of schooners and sloops, saw the
  ships at anchor,
The sailors at work in the rigging or out astride the spars,
The round masts, the swinging motion of the hulls, the
  slender serpentine pennants,
The large and small steamers in motion, the pilots in
  their pilot-houses,
The white wake left by the passage, the quick
  tremulous whirl of the wheels,
The flags of all nations, the falling of them at sunset,
The scallop-edged waves in the twilight, the ladled
  cups, the frolicsome crests and glistening,
The stretch afar growing dimmer and dimmer, the
  gray walls of the granite storehouses by the
  docks,
On the river the shadowy group, the big steam-tug
  closely flank'd on each side by the barges, the
  hay-boat, the belated lighter,
On the neighboring shore the fires from the foundry
  chimneys burning high and glaringly into the
  night,
Casting their flicker of black contrasted with wild red
  and yellow light over the tops of houses, and
  down into the clefts of streets.

4

These and all else were to me the same as they are
      to you,
I loved well those cities, loved well the stately and
      rapid river,
The men and women I saw were all near to me,
Others the same—others who look back on me because
      I look'd forward to them,
(The time will come, though I stop here to-day and
      to-night.)

What is it then between us?
What is the count of the scores or hundreds of years
      between us?

Whatever it is, it avails not—distance avails not, and
      place avails not,
I too lived, Brooklyn of ample hills was mine,
I too walk'd the streets of Manhattan island, and
      bathed in the waters around it,
I too felt the curious abrupt questionings stir
      within me,
In the day among crowds of people sometimes they
      came upon me,
In my walks home late at night or as I lay in my bed
      they came upon me,

I too had been struck from the float forever held in
    solution,
I too had receiv'd identity by my body,
That I was I knew was of my body, and what I should
    be I knew I should be of my body.

6

It is not upon you alone the dark patches fall,
The dark threw its patches down upon me also,
The best I had done seem'd to me blank and suspicious,
My great thoughts as I supposed them, were they not
    in reality meagre?
Nor is it you alone who know what it is to be evil,
I am he who knew what it was to be evil,
I too knitted the old knot of contrariety,
Blabb'd, blush'd, resented, lied, stole, grudg'd,
Had guile, anger, lust, hot wishes I dared not speak,
Was wayward, vain, greedy, shallow, sly, cowardly,
    malignant,
The wolf, the snake, the hog, not wanting in me,
The cheating look, the frivolous word, the adulterous
    wish, not wanting,
Refusals, hates, postponements, meanness, laziness,
    none of these wanting,
Was one with the rest, the days and haps of the rest,
Was call'd by my nighest name by clear loud voices of
    young men as they saw me approaching or passing,

Felt their arms on my neck as I stood, or the negligent
leaning of their flesh against me as I sat,
Saw many I loved in the street or ferry-boat or public
assembly, yet never told them a word,
Lived the same life with the rest, the same old
laughing, gnawing, sleeping,
Play'd the part that still looks back on the actor or actress,
The same old role, the role that is what we make it, as
great as we like,
Or as small as we like, or both great and small.

7

Closer yet I approach you,
What thought you have of me now, I had as much of
you—I laid in my stores in advance,
I consider'd long and seriously of you before you were
born.

Who was to know what should come home to me?
Who knows but I am enjoying this?
Who knows, for all the distance, but I am as good as
looking at you now, for all you cannot see me?

8

Ah, what can ever be more stately and admirable to me
than mast-hemm'd Manhattan?
River and sunset and scallop-edg'd waves of flood-tide?

The sea-gulls oscillating their bodies, the hay-boat in
the twilight, and the belated lighter?
What gods can exceed these that clasp me by the hand,
and with voices I love call me promptly and loudly
by my nighest name as I approach?
What is more subtle than this which ties me to the
woman or man that looks in my face?
Which fuses me into you now, and pours my meaning
into you?

We understand then do we not?
What I promis'd without mentioning it, have you not
accepted?
What the study could not teach—what the preaching
could not accomplish is accomplish'd, is it not?

9

Flow on, river! flow with the flood-tide, and ebb with
the ebb-tide!
Frolic on, crested and scallop-edg'd waves!
Gorgeous clouds of the sunset! drench with your
splendor me, or the men and women generations
after me!
Cross from shore to shore, countless crowds of
passengers!
Stand up, tall masts of Mannahatta! stand up, beautiful
hills of Brooklyn!

Throb, baffled and curious brain! throw out questions
and answers!

Suspend here and everywhere, eternal float of solution!

Gaze, loving and thirsting eyes, in the house or street
or public assembly!

Sound out, voices of young men! loudly and musically
call me by my nighest name!

Live, old life! play the part that looks back on the actor
or actress!

Play the old role, the role that is great or small
according as one makes it!

Consider, you who peruse me, whether I may not in
unknown ways be looking upon you;

Be firm, rail over the river, to support those who lean
idly, yet haste with the hasting current;

Fly on, sea birds! fly sideways, or wheel in large circles
high in the air;

Receive the summer sky, you water, and faithfully hold
it till all downcast eyes have time to take it from
you!

Diverge, fine spokes of light, from the shape of my
head, or any one's head, in the sunlit water!

Come on, ships from the lower bay! pass up or down,
white-sail'd schooners, sloops, lighters!

Flaunt away, flags of all nations! be duly lower'd at
sunset!

Burn high your fires, foundry chimneys! cast black

shadows at nightfall! cast red and yellow light
over the tops of the houses!
Appearances, now or henceforth, indicate what you are,
You necessary film, continue to envelop the soul,
About my body for me, and your body for you, be hung
our divinest aromas,
Thrive, cities—bring your freight, bring your shows,
ample and sufficient rivers,
Expand, being than which none else is perhaps more
spiritual,
Keep your places, objects than which none else is more
lasting.

You have waited, you always wait, you dumb, beautiful
ministers,
We receive you with free sense at last, and are insatiate
henceforward,
Not you any more shall be able to foil us, or withhold
yourselves from us,
We use you, and do not cast you aside—we plant you
permanently within us,
We fathom you not—we love you—there is perfection
in you also,
You furnish your parts toward eternity,
Great or small, you furnish your parts toward the soul.

THE HOUSE-TOP: A NIGHT PIECE
July, 1863—The Draft Riots

No sleep. The sultriness pervades the air
And binds the brain—a dense oppression, such
As tawny tigers feel in matted shades,
Vexing their blood and making apt for ravage.
Beneath the stars the roofy desert spreads
Vacant as Libya. All is hushed near by.
Yet fitfully from far breaks a mixed surf
Of muffled sound, the Atheist roar of riot.
Yonder, where parching Sirius set in drought,
Balefully glares red Arson—there—and there.
The Town is taken by its rats—ship-rats
And rats of the wharves. All Civil charms
And priestly spells which late held hearts in awe—
Fear-bound, subjected to a better sway
Than sway of self; these like a dream dissolve,
And man rebounds whole aeons back in nature.
Hail to the low dull rumble, dull and dead,
And ponderous drag that shakes the wall.
Wise Draco comes, deep in the midnight roll
Of black artillery; he comes, though late;
In code corroborating Calvin's creed
And cynic tyrannies of honest kings;
He comes, nor parleys; and the Town, redeemed,
Gives thanks devout; nor, being thankful, heeds

The grimy slur on the Republic's faith implied,
Which holds that Man is naturally good,
And—more—is Nature's Roman, never to be
    scourged.

THE TAXI

When I am away from you
The world beats dead
Like a slackened drum
I call out for you against the jutted stars
And shout into the ridges of the wind.
Streets coming fast,
One after the other,
Wedge you away from me,
And the lamps of the city prick my eyes
So that I can no longer see your face.
Why should I leave you,
To wound myself upon the sharp edges of the night?

ANTICIPATION

I have been temperate always,
But I am like to be very drunk
With your coming.
There have been times
I feared to walk down the street
Lest I should reel with the wine of you,
And jerk against my neighbors
As they go by.
I am parched now, and my tongue is horrible in
     my mouth,
But my brain is noisy
With the clash and gurgle of filling wine-cups.

ARRIVAL AT THE WALDORF

Home from Guatemala, back at the Waldorf.
This arrival in the wild country of the soul,
All approaches gone, being completely there,

Where the wild poem is a substitute
For the woman one loves or ought to love,
One wild rhapsody a fake for another.

You touch the hotel the way you touch light
Or sunlight and you hum and the orchestra
Hums and you say "The world in a verse,

A generation sealed, men remoter than mountains,
Women invisible in music and motion and color,"
After that alien, point-blank, green and actual
     Guatemala.

THE GREAT FIGURE

Among the rain
and lights
I saw a figure 5
in gold
on a red
firetruck
moving
tense
unheeded
to gong clangs
siren howls
and wheels rumbling
through the dark city.

UNION SQUARE

With the man I love who loves me not,
    I walked in the street-lamps' flare;
We watched the world go home that night
    In a flood through Union Square.

I leaned to catch the words he said
    That were light as a snowflake falling;
Ah well that he never leaned to hear
    The words my heart was calling.

And on we walked and on we walked
    Past the fiery lights of the picture shows—
Where the girls with thirsty eyes go by
    On the errand each man knows.

And on we walked and on we walked,
    At the door at last we said good-bye;
I knew by his smile he had not heard
    My heart's unuttered cry.

With the man I love who loves me not
    I walked in the street-lamps' flare—
But oh, the girls who can ask for love
    In the lights of Union Square.

BROADWAY

This is the quiet hour; the theaters
    Have gathered in their crowds, and steadily
    The million lights blaze on for few to see,
Robbing the sky of stars that should be hers.
A woman waits with bag and shabby furs,
    A somber man drifts by, and only we
    Pass up the street unwearied, warm and free,
For over us the olden magic stirs.
Beneath the liquid splendor of the lights
    We live a little ere the charm is spent;
This night is ours, of all the golden nights,
      The pavement an enchanted palace floor,
    And Youth the player on the viol, who sent
      A strain of music thru an open door.

NEW YORK

the savage's romance,
accreted where we need the space for commerce—
the centre of the wholesale fur trade,
starred with tepees of ermine and peopled with foxes,
the long guard-hairs waving two inches beyond the
    body of the pelt;
the ground dotted with deer-skins—white with white
    spots,
"as satin needlework in a single color may carry a
    varied pattern",
and wilting eagle's-down compacted by the wind;
and picardels of beaver-skin; white ones alert with
    snow.
It is a far cry from the "queen full of jewels"
and the beau with the muff,
from the gilt coach shaped like a perfume-bottle,
to the conjunction of the Monongahela and the
    Allegheny,
and the scholastic philosophy of the wilderness
to combat which one must stand outside and laugh
since to go in is to be lost.
It is not the dime-novel exterior,
Niagara Falls, the calico horses and the war-canoe;
It is not that "if the fur is not finer than such as one
    sees others wear,

one would rather be without it"—
that estimated in raw meat and berries, we could feed
    the universe;
it is not the atmosphere of ingenuity,
the otter, the beaver, the puma skins
without shooting-irons or dogs;
it is not the plunder,
but "accessibility to experience."

THE TROPICS IN NEW YORK

Bananas ripe and green, and ginger-root,
　　Cocoa in pods and alligator pears,
And tangerines and mangoes and grape fruit,
　　Fit for the highest prize at parish fairs,

Set in the window, bringing memories
　　Of fruit-trees laden by low-singing rills,
And dewy dawns, and mystical blue skies
　　In benediction over nun-like hills.

My eyes grew dim, and I could no more gaze;
　　A wave of longing through my body swept,
And, hungry for the old, familiar ways,
　　I turned aside and bowed my head and wept.

THE CITY'S LOVE

For one brief golden moment rare like wine,
The gracious city swept across the line;
Oblivious of the color of my skin,
Forgetting that I was an alien guest,
She bent to me, my hostile heart to win,
Caught me in passion to her pillowy breast.
The great, proud city, seized with a strange love,
Bowed down for one flame hour my pride to prove.

A SONG OF THE MOON

The moonlight breaks upon the city's domes,
And falls along cemented steel and stone,
Upon the grayness of a million homes,
Lugubrious in unchanging monotone.

Upon the clothes behind the tenement,
That hang like ghosts suspended from the lines,
Linking each flat, but to each indifferent,
Incongruous and strange the moonlight shines.

There is no magic from your presence here,
So moon, sad moon, tuck up your trailing robe,
Whose silver seems antique and too severe
Against the glow of one electric globe.

Go spill your beauty on the laughing faces
Of happy flowers that bloom a thousand hues,
Waiting on tiptoe in the wilding spaces,
To drink your wine mixed with sweet draughts
        of dews.

RECUERDO

We were very tired, we were very merry—
We had gone back and forth all night on the ferry.
It was bare and bright, and smelled like a stable—
But we looked into a fire, we leaned across a table,
We lay on a hill-top underneath the moon;
And the whistles kept blowing, and the dawn came
     soon.

We were very tired, we were very merry—
We had gone back and forth all night on the ferry;
And you ate an apple, and I ate a pear,
From a dozen of each we had bought somewhere;
And the sky went wan, and the wind came cold,
And the sun rose dripping, a bucketful of gold.

We were very tired, we were very merry,
We had gone back and forth all night on the ferry.
We hailed, "Good morrow, mother!" to a shawl-
     covered head,
And bought a morning paper, which neither of us read;
And she wept, "God bless you!" for the apples and
     pears,
And we gave her all our money but our subway fares.

"IF I SHOULD LEARN"

If I should learn, in some quite casual way,
    That you were gone, not to return again—
Read from the back-page of a paper, say,
    Held by a neighbor in a subway train,
How at the corner of this avenue
    And such a street (so are the papers filled)
A hurrying man—who happened to be you—
    At noon to-day had happened to be killed,
I should not cry aloud—I could not cry
    Aloud, or wring my hands in such a place—
I should but watch the station lights rush by
    With a more careful interest on my face,
Or raise my eyes and read with greater care
Where to store furs and how to treat the hair.

OBSERVATION

If I don't drive around the park,
I'm pretty sure to make my mark.
If I'm in bed each night by ten,
I may get back my looks again,
If I abstain from fun and such,
I'll probably amount to much,
But I shall stay the way I am,
Because I do not give a damn.

"TAXIS TOOT WHIRL PEOPLE MOVING"

taxis toot whirl people moving perhaps laugh into
        the slowly
millions and finally O it is spring since at all windows
microscopic birds sing fiercely two ragged men and a
filthiest woman busily are mending three wholly
        broken somehow
bowls or somethings by the web curb and carefully
        spring is
somehow skilfully everywhere mending smashed minds
O
the massacred gigantic world
again,into keen sunlight who lifts
glittering selfish new
limbs
and my heart stirs in his rags shaking from his
        armpits the
abundant lice of dreams laughing
rising sweetly out of the alive new mud my old
man heart striding shouts whimpers screams
        breathing into
his folded belly acres of sticky sunlight chatters bellows
swallowing globs of big life pricks wickedly his
mangled ears blinks into worlds of color shrieking
O begins
                the mutilated huge earth

again,up through darkness leaping
who sprints weirdly from its deep prison
groaning with perception and suddenly in all filthy
    alert things
which jumps mightily out of death
muscular,stinking,erect,entirely born.

"WALK ABOUT THE SUBWAY STATION"

Walk about the subway station
in a grove of steel pillars;
how their knobs, the rivet-heads—
unlike those of oaks—
are regularly placed;
how barren the ground is
except here and there on the platform
a flat black fungus
that was chewing-gum.

DAWN

Dawn in New York has
four columns of mire
and a hurricane of black pigeons
splashing in the putrid waters.
Dawn in New York groans
on enormous fire escapes
searching between the angles
for spikenards of drafted anguish.
Dawn arrives and no one receives it in his mouth
because morning and hope are impossible there:
sometimes the furious swarming coins
penetrate like drills and devour abandoned children.
Those who go out early know in their bones
there will be no paradise or loves that bloom and die:
they know they will be mired in numbers and laws,
in mindless games, in fruitless labors.
The light is buried under chains and noises
in an impudent challenge of rootless science.
And crowds stagger sleeplessly through the boroughs
as if they had just escaped a shipwreck of blood.

TO BROOKLYN BRIDGE

How many dawns, chill from his rippling rest
The seagull's wings shall dip and pivot him,
Shedding white rings of tumult, building high
Over the chained bay waters Liberty—

Then, with inviolate curve, forsake our eyes
As apparitional as sails that cross
Some page of figures to be filed away:
—Till elevators drop us from our day . . .

I think of cinemas, panoramic sleights
With multitudes bent toward some flashing scene
Never disclosed, but hastened to again,
Foretold to other eyes on the same screen;

And Thee, across the harbor, silver-paced
As though the sun took step of thee, yet left
Some motion ever unspent in thy stride,—
Implicitly thy freedom staying thee!

Out of some subway scuttle, cell or loft
A bedlamite speeds to thy parapets,
Tilting there momently, shrill shirt ballooning,
A jest falls from the speechless caravan.

Down Wall, from girder into street noon leaks,
A rip-tooth of the sky's acetylene;

All afternoon the cloud-flown derricks turn...
Thy cables breathe the North Atlantic still.

And obscure as that heaven of the Jews,
Thy guerdon ... Accolade thou dost bestow
Of anonymity time cannot raise:
Vibrant reprieve and pardon thou dost show.

O harp and altar, of the fury fused,
(How could mere toil align thy choiring strings!)
Terrific threshold of the prophet's pledge,
Prayer of pariah, and the lover's cry,—

Again the traffic lights that skim thy swift
Unfractioned idiom, immaculate sigh of stars,
Beading thy path—condense eternity:
And we have seen night lifted in thine arms.

Under thy shadow by the piers I waited;
Only in darkness is thy shadow clear.
The City's fiery parcels all undone,
Already snow submerges an iron year...

O Sleepless as the river under thee,
Vaulting the sea, the prairies' dreaming sod,
Unto us lowliest sometime sweep, descend
And of the curveship lend a myth to God.

THE HARBOR DAWN

Insistently through sleep—a tide of voices—
They meet you listening midway in your
    dream,
The long, tired sounds, fog-insulated noises:
Gongs in white surplices, beshrouded wails,
Far strum of fog horns . . . signals dispersed
    in veils.

*400 years and
more . . . or is
it from the
soundless shore
of sleep that
time*

And then a truck will lumber past the wharves
As winch engines begin throbbing on some deck;
Or a drunken stevedore's howl and thud below
Comes echoing alley-upward through dim snow.

And if they take your sleep away sometimes
They give it back again. Soft sleeves of sound
Attend the darkling harbor, the pillowed bay;
Somewhere out there in blankness steam

Spills into stream, and wanders, washed away
—Flurried by keen fifings, eddied
Among distant chiming buoys—adrift. The sky,
Cool feathery fold, suspends, distills
This wavering slumber. . . . Slowly—
Immemorially the window, the half-covered chair
Ask nothing but this sheath of pallid air.

And you beside me, blessèd now while sirens
Sing to us, stealthily weave us into day—
Serenely now, before day claims our eyes
Your cool arms murmurously about me lay.

recalls you to
your love,
there in a
waking dream
to merge
your seed

While myriad snowy hands are clustering at the panes—
        your hands within my hands are deeds;
        my tongue upon your throat—singing
        arms close; eyes wide, undoubtful
                dark
                        drink the dawn—
        a forest shudders in your hair!

The window goes blond slowly. Frostily clears. *—with whom?*
From Cyclopean towers across Manhattan
        waters
—Two—three bright window-eyes aglitter,
        disk
The sun, released—aloft with cold gulls hither.

The fog leans one last moment on the sill.
Under the mistletoe of dreams, a star—
As though to join us at some distant hill—
Turns in the waking west and goes to sleep.

Who is the
woman with
us in the
dawn?…
whose is the
flesh our feet
have moved
upon?

HART CRANE   57

THE TUNNEL

To Find the Western path
Right thro' the Gates of Wrath

BLAKE

Performances, assortments, résumés—
Up Times Square to Columbus Circle lights
Channel the congresses, nightly sessions,
Refractions of the thousand theatres, faces—
Mysterious kitchens. . . . You shall search them all.
Someday by heart you'll learn each famous sight
And watch the curtain lift in hell's despite;
You'll find the garden in the third act dead,
Finger your knees—and wish yourself in bed
With tabloid crime-sheets perched in easy sight.

> Then let you reach your hat
> and go.
> As usual, let you—also
> walking down—exclaim
> to twelve upward leaving
> a subscription praise
> for what time slays.

Or can't you quite make up your mind to ride;
A walk is better underneath the L a brisk

Ten blocks or so before? But you find yourself
Preparing penguin flexions of the arms,—
As usual you will meet the scuttle yawn:
The subway yawns the quickest promise home.

Be minimum, then, to swim the hiving swarms
Out of the Square, the Circle burning bright—
Avoid the glass doors gyring at your right,
Where boxed alone a second, eyes take fright
—Quite unprepared rush naked back to light:
And down beside the turnstile press the coin
Into the slot. The gongs already rattle.

      And so
      of cities you bespeak
      subways, rivered under streets
      and rivers.... In the car
      the overtone of motion
      underground, the monotone
      of motion is the sound
      of other faces, also underground—

"Let's have a pencil Jimmy—living now
at Floral Park
Flatbush—on the fourth of July—
like a pigeon's muddy dream—potatoes

to dig in the field—travlin the town—too—
night after night—the Culver line—the
girls all shaping up—it used to be—"

Our tongues recant like beaten weather vanes.
This answer lives like verdigris, like hair
Beyond extinction, surcease of the bone;
And repetition freezes—"What

"what do you want? getting weak on the links?
fandaddle daddy don't ask for change—IS THIS
FOURTEENTH? it's half past six she said—if
you don't like my gate why did you
swing on it, why *didja*
swing on it
anyhow—"

      And somehow anyhow swing—

The phonographs of hades in the brain
Are tunnels that re-wind themselves, and love
A burnt match skating in a urinal—
Somewhere above Fourteenth TAKE THE EXPRESS
To brush some new presentiment of pain—

"But I want service in this office SERVICE
 I said—after
the show she cried a little afterwards but—"

Whose head is swinging from the swollen strap?
Whose body smokes along the bitten rails,
Bursts from a smoldering bundle far behind
In back forks of the chasms of the brain,—
Puffs from a riven stump far out behind
In interborough fissures of the mind ...?

And why do I often meet your visage here,
Your eyes like agate lanterns—on and on
Below the toothpaste and the dandruff ads?
—And did their riding eyes right through your side,
And did their eyes like unwashed platters ride?
And Death, aloft,—gigantically down
Probing through you—toward me, O evermore!
And when they dragged your retching flesh,
Your trembling hands that night through Baltimore—
That last night on the ballot rounds, did you
Shaking, did you deny the ticket, Poe?

For Gravesend Manor change at Chambers Street.
The platform hurries along to a dead stop.

The intent escalator lifts a serenade
Stilly
Of shoes, umbrellas, each eye attending its shoe, then
Bolting outright somewhere above where streets
Burst suddenly in rain.... The gongs recur:
Elbows and levers, guard and hissing door.

Thunder is galvothermic here below.... The car
Wheels off. The train rounds, bending to a scream,
Taking the final level for the dive
Under the river—
And somewhat emptier than before,
Demented, for a hitching second, humps; then
Lets go.... Toward corners of the floor
Newspapers wing, revolve and wing.
Blank windows gargle signals through the roar.

And does the Dæmon take you home, also,
Wop washerwoman, with the bandaged hair?
After the corridors are swept, the cuspidors—
The gaunt sky-barracks cleanly now, and bare,
O Genoese, do you bring mother eyes and hands
Back home to children and to golden hair?

Dæmon, demurring and eventful yawn!
Whose hideous laughter is a bellows mirth
—Or the muffled slaughter of a day in birth—
O cruelly to inoculate the brinking dawn
With antennae toward worlds that glow and sink;—
To spoon us out more liquid than the dim
Locution of the eldest star, and pack
The conscience navelled in the plunging wind,
Umbilical to call—and straightway die!

O caught like pennies beneath soot and steam,

Kiss of our agony thou gatherest;
Condensed, thou takest all—shrill ganglia
Impassioned with some song we fail to keep.
And yet, like Lazarus, to feel the slope,
The sod and billow breaking,—lifting ground,
—A sound of waters bending astride the sky
Unceasing with some Word that will not die . . . !

*   *   *

A tugboat, wheezing wreaths of steam,
Lunged past, with one galvanic blare stove up the
    River.
I counted the echoes assembling, one after one,
Searching, thumbing the midnight on the piers.
Lights, coasting, left the oily tympanum of waters;
The blackness somewhere gouged glass on a sky.
And this thy harbor, O my City, I have driven under,
Tossed from the coil of ticking towers. . . . Tomorrow,
And to be. . . . Here by the River that is East—
Here at the waters' edge the hands drop memory;
Shadowless in that abyss they unaccounting lie.
How far away the star has pooled the sea—
Or shall the hands be drawn away, to die?

Kiss of our agony Thou gatherest,
                O Hand of Fire
                        gatherest—

THE WEARY BLUES

Droning a drowsy syncopated tune,
Rocking back and forth to a mellow croon,
    I heard a Negro play.
Down on Lenox Avenue the other night
By the pale dull pallor of an old gas light
    He did a lazy sway. . . .
    He did a lazy sway. . . .
To the tune o' those Weary Blues.
With his ebony hands on each ivory key
He made that poor piano moan with melody.
    O Blues!
Swaying to and fro on his rickety stool
He played that sad raggy tune like a musical fool.
    Sweet Blues!
Coming from a black man's soul.
    O Blues!
In a deep song voice with a melancholy tone
I heard that Negro sing, that old piano moan—
    "Ain't got nobody in all this world,
    Ain't got nobody but ma self.
    I's gwine to quit ma frownin'
    And put ma troubles on the shelf."
Thump, thump, thump, went his foot on the floor.
He played a few chords then he sang some more—

> "I got the Weary Blues
> And I can't be satisfied.
> Got the Weary Blues
> And can't be satisfied—
> I ain't happy no mo'
> And I wish that I had died."
And far into the night he crooned that tune.
The stars went out and so did the moon.
The singer stopped playing and went to bed
While the Weary Blues echoed through his head.
He slept like a rock, or a man that's dead.

LANGSTON HUGHES

GOOD MORNING

Good morning, daddy!
I was born here, he said,
watched Harlem grow
until colored folks spread
from river to river
across the middle of Manhattan
out of Penn Station
dark tenth of a nation,
planes from Puerto Rico,
and holds of boats, chico,
up from Cuba Haiti Jamaica,
in buses marked New York
from Georgia Florida Louisiana
to Harlem Brooklyn the Bronx
but most of all to Harlem
dusky sash across Manhattan
I've seen them come dark
    wondering
    wide-eyed
    dreaming
out of Penn Station—
but the trains are late.
The gates open—
Yet there're bars
at each gate.

What happens
to a dream deferred?

Daddy, ain't you heard?

HARLEM

What happens to a dream deferred?

Does it dry up
like a raisin in the sun?
Or fester like a sore—
And then run?
Does it stink like rotten meat?
Or crust and sugar over—
like a syrupy sweet?

Maybe it just sags
like a heavy load.

Or does it explode?

JUKE BOX LOVE SONG

I could take the Harlem night
and wrap around you,
Take the neon lights and make a crown,
Take the Lenox Avenue busses,
Taxis, subways,
And for your love song tone their rumble down.
Take Harlem's heartbeat,
Make a drumbeat,
Put it on a record, let it whirl,
And while we listen to it play,
Dance with you till day—
Dance with you, my sweet brown Harlem girl.

SUBWAY RUSH HOUR

Mingled
breath and smell
so close
mingled
black and white
so near
no room for fear.

THE STREET TO THE
ESTABLISHMENT

You're the old. I'm the new
I'm the multi. You're the few
You're the gained, the attained,
the begun, the become,
the prize that's been won
the picked from the which.
You're part of the mural on the wall,
the spire that cannot fall.
I'm the aborted
I'm the itch.

REFUGEE BLUES

Say this city has ten million souls,
Some are living in mansions, some are living in holes:
Yet there's no place for us, my dear, yet there's no
    place for us.

Once we had a country and we thought it fair,
Look in the atlas and you'll find it there:
We cannot go there now, my dear, we cannot go
    there now.

In the village churchyard there grows an old yew,
Every spring it blossoms anew:
Old passports can't do that, my dear, old passports
    can't do that.

The consul banged the table and said,
"If you've got no passport you're officially dead":
But we are still alive, my dear, but we are still alive.

Went to a committee; they offered me a chair;
Asked me politely to return next year:
But where shall we go to-day, my dear, but where shall
    we go to-day?

Came to a public meeting; the speaker got up and said,
"If we let them in, they will steal our daily bread":

He was talking of you and me, my dear, he was talking
    of you and me.

Thought I heard the thunder rumbling in the sky;
It was Hitler over Europe, saying, "They must die":
O we were in his mind, my dear, O we were in his mind.

Saw a poodle in a jacket fastened with a pin,
Saw a door opened and a cat let in:
But they weren't German Jews, my dear, but they
    weren't German Jews.

Went down the harbor and stood upon the quay,
Saw the fish swimming as if they were free:
Only ten feet away, my dear, only ten feet away.

Walked through a wood, saw the birds in the trees;
They had no politicians and sang at their ease:
They weren't the human race, my dear, they weren't
    the human race.

Dreamed I saw a building with a thousand floors,
A thousand windows and a thousand doors:
Not one of them was ours, my dear, not one of them
    was ours.

Stood on a great plain in the falling snow;
Ten thousand soldiers marched to and fro:
Looking for you and me, my dear, looking for you
    and me.

W. H. AUDEN   71

SEPTEMBER 1, 1939

I sit in one of the dives
On Fifty-Second Street
Uncertain and afraid
As the clever hopes expire
Of a low dishonest decade:
Waves of anger and fear
Circulate over the bright
And darkened lands of the earth,
Obsessing our private lives;
The unmentionable odour of death
Offends the September night.

Accurate scholarship can
Unearth the whole offence
From Luther until now
That has driven a culture mad,
Find what occurred at Linz,
What huge imago made
A psychopathic god:
I and the public know
What all schoolchildren learn,
Those to whom evil is done
Do evil in return.

Exiled Thucydides knew
All that a speech can say
About Democracy,
And what dictators do,
The elderly rubbish they talk
To an apathetic grave;
Analysed all in his book,
The enlightenment driven away,
The habit-forming pain,
Mismanagement and grief:
We must suffer them all again.

Into this neutral air
Where blind skyscrapers use
Their full height to proclaim
The strength of Collective Man,
Each language pours its vain
Competitive excuse:
But who can live for long
In an euphoric dream;
Out of the mirror they stare,
Imperialism's face
And the international wrong.

Faces along the bar
Cling to their average day:
The lights must never go out,
The music must always play,
All the conventions conspire
To make this fort assume
The furniture of home;
Lest we should see where we are,
Lost in a haunted wood,
Children afraid of the night
Who have never been happy or good.

The windiest militant trash
Important Persons shout
Is not so crude as our wish:
What mad Nijinsky wrote
About Diaghilev
Is true of the normal heart;
For the error bred in the bone
Of each woman and each man
Craves what it cannot have,
Not universal love
But to be loved alone.

From the conservative dark
Into the ethical life
The dense commuters come,
Repeating their morning vow,
"I *will* be true to the wife,
I'll concentrate more on my work,"
And helpless governors wake
To resume their compulsory game:
Who can release them now,
Who can reach the deaf,
Who can speak for the dumb?

All I have is a voice
To undo the folded lie,
The romantic lie in the brain
Of the sensual man-in-the-street
And the lie of Authority
Whose buildings grope the sky:
There is no such thing as the State
And no one exists alone;
Hunger allows no choice
To the citizen or the police;
We must love one another or die.

Defenceless under the night
Our world in stupor lies;
Yet, dotted everywhere,
Ironic points of light
Flash out wherever the Just
Exchange their messages:
May I, composed like them
Of Eros and of dust,
Beleaguered by the same
Negation and despair,
Show an affirming flame.

W. H. AUDEN

PEDESTRIAN

What generations could have dreamed
This grandchild of the shopping streets, her eyes

In the buyer's light, the store lights
Brighter than the lighthouses, brighter than moonrise

From the salt harbor so rich
So bright her city

In a soil of pavement, a mesh of wires where she walks
In the new winter among enormous buildings.

THE MAN-MOTH*

　　　　　Here, above,
cracks in the buildings are filled with battered moonlight.
The whole shadow of Man is only as big as his hat.
It lies at his feet like a circle for a doll to stand on,
and he makes an inverted pin, the point magnetized to
　　　the moon.
He does not see the moon; he observes only her vast
　　　properties,
feeling the queer light on his hands, neither warm
　　　nor cold,
of a temperature impossible to record in thermometers.

　　　　　But when the Man-Moth
pays his rare, although occasional, visits to the surface,
the moon looks rather different to him. He emerges
from an opening under the edge of one of the sidewalks
and nervously begins to scale the faces of the buildings.
He thinks the moon is a small hole at the top of the sky,
proving the sky quite useless for protection.
He trembles, but must investigate as high as he can
　　　climb.

*Newspaper misprint for "mammoth."

Up the façades,
his shadow dragging like a photographer's cloth behind
    him,
he climbs fearfully, thinking that this time he will manage
to push his small head through that round clean opening
and be forced through, as from a tube, in black scrolls on
    the light.
(Man, standing below him, has no such illusions.)
But what the Man-Moth fears most he must do, although
he fails, of course, and falls back scared but quite unhurt.

Then he returns
to the pale subways of cement he calls his home. He flits,
he flutters, and cannot get aboard the silent trains
fast enough to suit him. The doors close swiftly.
The Man-Moth always seats himself facing the wrong
    way
and the train starts at once at its full, terrible speed,
without a shift in gears or a gradation of any sort.
He cannot tell the rate at which he travels backwards.

Each night he must
be carried through artificial tunnels and dream
    recurrent dreams.
Just as the ties recur beneath his train, these underlie

his rushing brain. He does not dare look out the window,
for the third rail, the unbroken draught of poison,
runs there beside him. He regards it as a disease
he has inherited the susceptibility to. He has to keep
his hands in his pockets, as others must wear mufflers.

                If you catch him,
hold up a flashlight to his eye. It's all dark pupil,
an entire night itself, whose haired horizon tightens
as he stares back, and closes up the eye. Then from the lids
one tear, his only possession, like the bee's sting, slips.
Slyly he palms it, and if you're not paying attention
he'll swallow it. However, if you watch, he'll hand it over,
cool as from underground springs and pure enough
    to drink.

LETTER TO N.Y.
For Louise Crane

In your next letter I wish you'd say
where you are going and what you are doing;
how are the plays, and after the plays
what other pleasures you're pursuing:

taking cabs in the middle of the night,
driving as if to save your soul
where the road goes round and round the park
and the meter glares like a moral owl,

and the trees look so queer and green
standing alone in big black caves
and suddenly you're in a different place
where everything seems to happen in waves,

and most of the jokes you just can't catch,
like dirty words rubbed off a slate,
and the songs are loud but somehow dim
and it gets so terribly late,

and coming out of the brownstone house
to the gray sidewalk, the watered street,
one side of the buildings rises with the sun
like a glistening field of wheat.

—Wheat, not oats, dear. I'm afraid
if it's wheat it's none of your sowing,
nevertheless I'd like to know
what you are doing and where you are going.

SEVENTH AVENUE

This is the cripples' hour on Seventh Avenue
when they emerge, the two o'clock night-walkers,
the cane, the crutch, and the black suit.

Oblique early mirages send the eyes:
light dramatized in puddles, the animal glare
that makes indignity, makes the brute.

Not enough effort in the sky for morning.
No color, pantomime of blackness, landscape
where the third layer back is always phantom.

Here comes the fat man, the attractive dog-chested
legless—and the wounded infirm king
with nobody to use him as a saint.

Now they parade in the dark, the cripples' hour
to the drugstore, the bar, the newspaper-stand,
past kissing shadows on a window-shade to

colors of alcohol, reflectors, light.
Wishing for trial to prove their innocence
with one straight simple look:

the look to set this avenue in its colors—
two o'clock on a black street instead of
wounds, mysteries, fables, kings
in a kingdom of cripples.

MURIEL RUKEYSER   83

STAYING AT ED'S PLACE

I like being in your apartment, and no disturbing
        anything.
As in the woods I wouldn't want to move a tree,
or change the play of sun and shadow on the ground.

The yellow kitchen stool belongs right there
against white plaster. I haven't used your purple towel
because I like the accidental cleft of shade you left in it.

At your small six-sided table, covered with mysterious
dents in the wood like a dartboard, I drink my coffee
from your brown mug. I look into the clearing

of your high front room, where sunlight slopes
        through bare
window squares. Your Afghanistan hammock,
        a man-sized cocoon
slung from wall to wall, your narrow desk and
        typewriter

are the only furniture. Each morning your light from
        the east
douses me where, with folded legs, I sit in your
        meadow,
a casual spread of brilliant carpets. Like a cat or dog

I take a roll, then, stretched out flat
in the center of color and pattern, I listen
to the remote growl of trucks over cobbles on Bethune
     Street below.

When I open my eyes I discover the peaceful blank
of the ceiling. Its old paint-layered surface is
     moonwhite
and trackless, like the Sea——of Tranquillity.

AT THE MUSEUM OF MODERN ART

At the Museum of Modern Art you can sit in the lobby
on the foam-rubber couch; you can rest and smoke,
and view whatever the revolving doors express.
You don't have to go into the galleries at all.

In this arena the exhibits are free and have all
the surprises of art—besides something extra:
sensory restlessness, the play of alternation,
expectation in an incessant spray

thrown from heads, hands, the tendons of ankles.
The shifts and strollings of feet
engender compositions on the shining tiles,
and glide together and pose gambits,

gestures of design, that scatter, rearrange,
trickle into lines, and turn clicking through a wicket
into rooms where caged colors blotch the walls.
You don't have to go to the movie downstairs

to sit on red plush in the snow and fog
of old-fashioned silence. You can see contemporary
Garbos and Chaplins go by right here.
And there's a mesmeric experimental film

constantly reflected on the flat side of the wide
steel-plate pillar opposite the crenellated window.
Non-objective taxis surging west, on Fifty-third,
liquefy in slippery yellows, dusky crimsons,

pearly mauves—an accelerated sunset, a roiled
surf, or cloud-curls undulating—their tubular ribbons
elongations of the coils of light itself
(engine of color) and motion (motor of form).

FUTURE-PRESENT

Remember the old days when the luxury liners
                 in narrow Manhattan
appeared piecemeal in segments at the end of east-west
                 streets,
a black-and-white section of portholes and stripes of
     decks
and slowly the majesty of the great red funnel,
even the olympian basso of its homing horn?
It would take a full half hour to go past,
as if in no hurry to pass into history.

But look there at the top pane of the window!
A burnished skyliner elegantly moving north,
as proud as leviathan above the suffering Hudson,
past the unfinished cathedral, over Grant's tomb,
into the blue-gray morning of the future-present.

"THE PENNYCANDYSTORE BEYOND THE EL"

The Pennycandystore beyond the El
is where I first
                    fell in love
                              with unreality
Jellybeans glowed in the semi-gloom
of that september afternoon
A cat upon the counter moved among
                              the licorice sticks
              and tootsie rolls
          and Oh Boy Gum

Outside the leaves were falling as they died

A wind had blown away the sun

A girl ran in
Her hair was rainy
Her breasts were breathless in the little room

Outside the leaves were falling
                              and they cried
                                        Too soon! too soon!

LAWRENCE FERLINGHETTI   89

DANCERS EXERCISING

Frame within frame, the evolving conversation
is dancelike, as though two could play
at improvising snowflakes'
six-feather-vaned evanescence,
no two ever alike. All process
and no arrival: the happier we are,
the less there is for memory to take hold of,
or—memory being so largely a predilection
for the exceptional—come to a halt
in front of. But finding, one evening
on a street not quite familiar,
inside a gated
November-sodden garden, a building
of uncertain provenance,
peering into whose vestibule we were
arrested—a frame within a frame,
a lozenge of impeccable clarity—
by the reflection, no, not
of our two selves, but of
dancers exercising in a mirror,
at the center
of that clarity, what we saw
was not stillness
but movement: the perfection
of memory consisting, it would seem,

in the never-to-be-completed.
We saw them mirroring themselves,
never guessing the vestibule
that defined them, frame within frame,
contained two other mirrors.

THE NATURE OF THIS CITY

Children walking with their grandmothers
talk foreign languages
that is the nature of this city
and also this country

Talk is cheap but comes in variety
and witnessing dialect
there is a rule for all
and in each sentence a perfect grammar

FEAR

I am afraid of nature
because of nature   I am mortal

my children and my grandchildren
are also mortal

I lived in the city for forty years
in this way I escaped fear

ON MOTHER'S DAY

I went out walking
in the old neighborhood

Look! more trees on the block
forget-me-nots all around them
ivy   lantana shining
and geraniums in the window

Twenty years ago
it was believed that the roots of trees
would insert themselves into gas lines
then fall   poisoned   on houses and children

or tap the city's water pipes   starved
for nitrogen   obstruct the sewers

In those days in the afternoon I floated
by ferry to Hoboken or Staten Island
then pushed the babies in their carriages
along the river wall   observing Manhattan
See Manhattan I cried   New York!
even at sunset it doesn't shine
but stands in fire   charcoal to the waist

But this Sunday afternoon on Mother's Day
I walked west   and came to Hudson Street
      tricolored flags
were flying over old oak furniture for sale
brass bedsteads   copper pots and vases
by the pound from India

Suddenly before my eyes   twenty-two transvestites
in joyous parade stuffed pillows
under their lovely gowns
and entered a restaurant
under a sign which said   All Pregnant Mothers Free

I watched them place napkins over their bellies
and accept coffee and zabaglione

I am especially open to sadness and hilarity
since my father died as a child
one week ago in this his ninetieth year

THE BUILDING

Removed by half a city, not the world,
I see the building you are working in.
It is a winter day. The branches clash
On the few trees that mark the avenue.
If I could go to where I wanted to,
How would I find you? As you were before?
Or are you like the person I've become,
Far into the dark, and far from home?

This winter day was not so dark before
That light was lost that only you could know.
When I go home, and then the dark comes home,
The branches clash along the avenue.
If you could go, I think I'd want you to,
Somewhere the building you'd be working in
Would be a world away, and far from home.
I'm far into the dark when far from you,

And this is something only you could know:
I'm not the person that I was before
You went into the dark. In finding you,
I used to go just where I wanted to.
On the few trees that mark the avenue
The branches clash. It is a winter day.
I see the building you are working in
Removed by half a city, and the world.

HOWARD MOSS   95

THE ROOF GARDEN

A nervous hose is dribbling on the tar
This morning on this rooftop where I'm watching you
Move among your sparse, pinchpenny flowers,
Poor metronomes of color one month long
That pull the sun's rays in as best they can
And suck life up from one mere inch of dirt.
There's water in the sky but it won't come down.
Once we counted the skyline's water towers,
Barrels made of shingle, fat and high,
An African village suspended above
The needle hardness of New York that needs
More light than God provides to make it soft,
That needs the water in the water towers
To snake through pipe past all the elevators
To open up in bowls and baths and showers.

Soon our silence will dissolve in talk,
In talk that needs some water and some sun,
Or it will go the same way as before:
Dry repetitions of the ill we bear
Each other, the baited poles of light
Angling through the way the sun today
Fishes among the clouds.

Now you are through
Watering geraniums and now you go
To the roof edge to survey the real estate
Of architectural air—tense forms wrought up,
Torn down, replaced, to be torn down again . . .
So much like us. Your head against the sky
Is topped by a tower clock, blocks away,
Whose two black hands are closing on the hour,
And I look down into the street below,
Rinsed fresh this morning by a water truck,
Down which a girl, perky in high heels,
Clops by, serenely unaware of us,
Of the cables, gas lines, telephone wires,
And water mains, writhing underfoot.

THE CABDRIVER'S SMILE

Tough guy. Star of David
and something in Hebrew—a motto—
hang where Catholics used to dangle
St. Christopher (now discredited).
No smile. White hair. American-born,
I'd say, maybe the Bronx.
When another cab pulls alongside
at a light near the Midtown Tunnel, and its driver
rolls down his window and greets this guy
with a big happy face and a first-name greeting,
he bows like a king, a formal acknowledgement,
and to me remarks,

          deadpan,
       "Seems to think he knows me."

"You mean you don't know him?"—I lean forward
    laughing,
close to the money-window.

              "Never seen him before in my life."
Something like spun steel floats invisible, until

                     questions strike it,
all round him, the way light gleams webs among
                    grass in fall.
And on we skim
in silence past the cemeteries, into

the airport, ahead of time. He's beat
the afternoon traffic. I tip him well.
A cool acceptance. Cool? It's
cold as ice.
          Yet I've seen,
squinting to read his license,
how he smiled—timidly?—anyway,
smiled, as if hoping to please,
at the camera. My heart
stabs me. Somewhere this elderly
close-mouthed skeptic hides
longing and hope. Wanted
—immortalized for the cops, for his fares, for the world—
to be looking his best.

THIS DARK APARTMENT

Coming from the deli
a block away today I
saw the UN building
shine and in all the
months and years I've
lived in this apartment
I took so you and I
would have a place to
meet I never noticed
that it was in my view.

I remember very well
the morning I walked in
and found you in bed
with X. He dressed
and left. You dressed
too. I said, "Stay
five minutes." You
did. You said, "That's
the way it is." It
was not much of a surprise.

Then X got on speed
and ripped off an
antique chest and an

air conditioner, etc.
After he was gone and
you had changed the
Segal lock, I asked
you on the phone, "Can't
you be content with
your wife and me?" "I'm
not built that way,"
you said. No surprise.

Now, without saying
why, you've let me go.
You don't return my
calls, who used to call
me almost every evening
when I lived in the coun-
try. "Hasn't he told you
why?" "No, and I doubt he
ever will." Goodbye. It's
mysterious and frustrating.

How I wish you would come
back! I could tell
you how, when I lived
on East 49th, first

with Frank and then with John,
we had a lovely view of
the UN building and the
Beekman Towers. They were
not my lovers, though.
You were. You said so.

AN EAST WINDOW ON ELIZABETH STREET

For Bob Dash

Among the silvery, the dulled sparkling mica lights of
      tar roofs
lie rhizomes of wet under an iris
from a bargain nursery sky: a feeble blue with skim
      milk blotched
on the falls. Junky buildings, aligned by a child
("That's very good, dear") are dental:
carious, and the color of weak gums ("Rinse and spit"
and blood stained sputum and big gritty bits
are swirled away). Across an interstice
trundle and trot trucks, cabs, cars,
station-bound fat dressy women
("I never thought I'd make it")
all foundation garments and pinched toes. I don't know
      how
it can look so miraculous and alive
an organic skin for the stacked cubes of air
people need, things forcing up through the thick
      unwilling air
obstinate and mindless as the glorious swamp flower
skunk cabbage and the tight uncurling punchboard slips
of fern fronds. Toned, like patched, wash-faded rags.
Noble and geometric, like Laurana's project for a square.

Mutable, delicate, expendable, ugly, mysterious
(seven stories of just bathroom windows)
packed: a man asleep, a woman slicing garlic thinly
      into oil
(what a stink, what a wonderful smell)
burgeoning with stacks, pipes, ventilators, tensile
      antennae—
that bristling gray bit is a part of a bridge,
that mesh hangar on a roof is to play games under.
But why should a metal ladder climb, straight
and sky aspiring, five rungs above a stairway hood
up into nothing? Out there
a bird is building a nest out of torn up letters
and the red cellophane off cigarette and gum packs.
The furthest off people are tiny as fine seed
but not at all bug like. A pinprick of blue
plainly is a child running.

MARCH HERE

Wet
     the tide out
DONALD'S GARAGE
                    neon sign
left on all night
      a red pulse
   pale
under the skin
     throbs
                  when you turn your head
  light
     tall in the sky
walks over towers
              the hard-running river
    in your neck
    the steady pulse
  gently beats
                          damp
            from your bath
             your body
exhales a soft wet smell
                    of March

PHOTOGRAPH FROM SEPTEMBER 11

They jumped from the burning floors—
one, two, a few more,
higher, lower.

The photograph halted them in life,
and now keeps them
above the earth toward the earth.

Each is still complete,
with a particular face
and blood well-hidden.

There's enough time
for hair to come loose,
for keys and coins
to fall from pockets.

They're still within the air's reach,
in the compass of places
that have just now opened.

I can do only two things for them—
describe this flight
and not add a last line.

106 WISLAWA SZYMBORSKA
       TRANSLATED BY STANISLAW BARANCZAK
       AND CLARE CAVANAGH

GIRL AND BABY FLORIST SIDEWALK
PRAM NINETEEN SEVENTY SOMETHING

Sweeping past the florist's came the baby and the girl
I am the girl! I am the baby!
I am the florist who is filled with mood!
I am the mood. I am the girl who is inside the baby
For it is a baby girl. I am old style of life. I am the new
Everything as well. I am the evening in which you
     docked your first kiss.
And it came to the baby. And I am the boyhood of
     the girl
Which she never has. I am the florist's unknown baby
He hasn't had one yet. The florist is in a whirl
So much excitement, section, outside his shop
Or hers. Who is he? Where goes the baby? She
Is immensely going to grow up. How much
Does this rent for? It's more than a penny. It's more
Than a million cents. My dear, it is life itself. Roses?
Chrysanthemums? If you can't buy them I'll give
Them for nothing. Oh no, I can't.
Maybe my baby is allergic to their spores.
So then the girl and her baby go away. Florist stands
     whistling
Neither inside nor outside thinking about the
     mountains of Peru.

96 VANDAM

I am going to carry my bed into New York City tonight
complete with dangling sheets and ripped blankets;
I am going to push it across three dark highways
or coast along under 600,000 faint stars.
I want to have it with me so I don't have to beg
for too much shelter from my weak and exhausted
          friends.
I want to be as close as possible to my pillow
in case a dream or a fantasy should pass by.
I want to fall asleep on my own fire escape
and wake up dazed and hungry
to the sound of garbage grinding in the street below
and the smell of coffee cooking in the window above.

LET ME PLEASE LOOK INTO
MY WINDOW

Let me please look into my window on 103rd Street
    one more time—
without crying, without tearing the satin, without
    touching
the white face, without straightening the tie or
    crumpling the flower.

Let me walk up Broadway past Zak's, past the Melody
    Fruit Store,
past Stein's Eyes, past the New Moon Inn, past the
    Olympia.

Let me leave quietly by gate 29
and fall asleep as we pull away from the ramp
into the tunnel.

Let me wake up happy, let me know where I am, let me
    lie still,
as we turn left, as we cross the water, as we leave the
    light.

GERALD STERN   109

STEPS

How funny you are today New York
like Ginger Rogers in *Swingtime*
and St. Bridget's steeple leaning a little to the left

here I have just jumped out of a bed full of V-days
(I got tired of D-days) and blue you there still
accepts me foolish and free
all I want is a room up there
and you in it
and even the traffic halt so thick is a way
for people to rub up against each other
and when their surgical appliances lock
they stay together
for the rest of the day (what a day)
I go by to check a slide and I say
that painting's not so blue
where's Lana Turner
she's out eating
and Garbo's backstage at the Met
everyone's taking their coat off
so they can show a rib-cage to the rib-watchers
and the park's full of dancers with their tights and shoes
in little bags
who are often mistaken for worker-outers at the
          West Side Y

why not
the Pittsburgh Pirates shout because they won
and in a sense we're all winning
we're alive

the apartment was vacated by a gay couple
who moved to the country for fun
they moved a day too soon
even the stabbings are helping the population explosion
though in the wrong country
and all those liars have left the UN
the Seagram Building's no longer rivalled in interest
not that we need liquor (we just like it)

and the little box is out on the sidewalk
next to the delicatessen
so the old man can sit on it and drink beer
and get knocked off it by his wife later in the day
while the sun is still shining

oh god it's wonderful
to get out of bed
and drink too much coffee
and smoke too many cigarettes
and love you so much

GAMIN

All the roofs are wet
and underneath smoke
that piles softly in
streets, tongues are
on top of each other
mulling over the night.

We lay against each other
like banks of violets
while the slate slips
off the roof into the
garden of the old lady
next door. She is my

enemy. She hates cats
airplanes and my self
as if we were memories
of war. Bah! when you
are close I thumb my
nose at her and laugh.

AN URBAN CONVALESCENCE

Out for a walk, after a week in bed,
I find them tearing up part of my block
And, chilled through, dazed and lonely, join the dozen
In meek attitudes, watching a huge crane
Fumble luxuriously in the filth of years.
Her jaws dribble rubble. An old man
Laughs and curses in her brain,
Bringing to mind the close of *The White Goddess.*

As usual in New York, everything is torn down
Before you have had time to care for it.
Head bowed, at the shrine of noise, let me try to recall
What building stood here. Was there a building at all?
I have lived on this same street for a decade.

Wait. Yes. Vaguely a presence rises
Some five floors high, of shabby stone
—Or am I confusing it with another one
In another part of town, or of the world?—
And over its lintel into focus vaguely
Misted with blood (my eyes are shut)
A single garland sways, stone fruit, stone leaves,
Which years of grit had etched until it thrust
Roots down, even into the poor soil of my seeing.
When did the garland become part of me?

I ask myself, amused almost,
Then shiver once from head to toe,

Transfixed by a particular cheap engraving of garlands
Bought for a few francs long ago,
All calligraphic tendril and cross-hatched rondure,
Ten years ago, and crumpled up to stanch
Boughs dripping, whose white gestures filled a cab,
And thought of neither then nor since.
Also, to clasp them, the small, red-nailed hand
Of no one I can place. Wait. No. Her name, her features
Lie toppled underneath that year's fashions.
The words she must have spoken, setting her face
To fluttering like a veil, I cannot hear now,
Let alone understand.

So that I am already on the stair,
As it were, of where I lived,
When the whole structure shudders at my tread
And soundlessly collapses, filling
The air with motes of stone.
Onto the still erect building next door
Are pressed levels and hues—
Pocked rose, streaked greens, brown whites.
Who drained the pousse-café?
Wires and pipes, snapped off at the roots, quiver.

Well, that is what life does. I stare
A moment longer, so. And presently
The massive volume of the world
Closes again.

Upon that book I swear
To abide by what it teaches:
Gospels of ugliness and waste,
Of towering voids, of soiled gusts,
Of a shrieking to be faced
Full into, eyes astream with cold—

With cold?
All right then. With self-knowledge.

Indoors at last, the pages of *Time* are apt
To open, and the illustrated mayor of New York,
Given a glimpse of how and where I work,
To note yet one more house that can be scrapped.

Unwillingly I picture
My walls weathering in the general view.
It is not even as though the new
Buildings did very much for architecture.

Suppose they did. The sickness of our time requires
That these as well be blasted in their prime.

You would think the simple fact of having lasted
Threatened our cities like mysterious fires.

There are certain phrases which to use in a poem
Is like rubbing silver with quicksilver. Bright
But facile, the glamour deadens overnight.
For instance, how "the sickness of our time"

Enhances, then debases, what I feel.
At my desk I swallow in a glass of water
No longer cordial, scarcely wet, a pill
They had told me not to take until much later.

With the result that back into my imagination
The city glides, like cities seen from the air,
Mere smoke and sparkle to the passenger
Having in mind another destination

Which now is not that honey-slow descent
Of the Champs-Elysées, her hand in his,
But the dull need to make some kind of house
Out of the life lived, out of the love spent.

These city apartment windows—my grandmother's
    once—
Must be replaced come Fall at great expense.
Pre-war sun shone through them on many a Saturday
Lunch unconsumed while frantic adolescence
Wheedled an old lady into hat and lipstick,
Into her mink, the taxi, the packed lobby,
Into our seats. Whereupon gold curtains parted
On Lakmé's silvery, not yet broken-hearted

Version of things as they were. But what remains
Exactly as it was except those panes?
Today's memo from the Tenants' Committee deplores
Even the ongoing deterioration
Of the *widows* in our building. Well. On the bright side,
Heating costs and street noise will be cut.
Sirens at present like intergalactic gay
Bars in full swing whoop past us night and day.

Sometimes, shocked wide awake, I've tried to reckon
How many lives—fifty, a hundred thousand?—
Are being shortened by that din of crosstown
Ruby flares, wherever blinds don't quite . . .
And shortened by how much? Ten minutes each?
Reaching the Emergency Room alive, the victim

Would still have to live *years*, just to repair
The sonic fallout of a single scare.

"Do you ever wonder where you'll—" Oh my dear,
Asleep somewhere, or at the wheel. Not here.
Within months of the bathroom ceiling's cave-in,
Which missed my grandmother by a white hair,
She moved back South. The point's to live in style,
Not to drop dead in it. On a carpet of flowers
Nine levels above ground, like Purgatory,
Our life is turning into a whole new story:

Juices, blue cornbread, afternoons at the gym—
Imagine who remembers how to swim!
Evenings of study, or intensive care
For one another. Early to bed. And later,
If the mirror's drowsy eye perceives a slight
But brilliant altercation between curtains
Healed by the leaden hand of—one of us?
A white-haired ghost? or the homunculus

A gentle alchemist behind them trains
To put in order these nocturnal scenes—
Two heads already featureless in gloom
Have fallen back to sleep. Tomorrow finds me
Contentedly playing peekaboo with a sylphlike
Quirk in the old glass, making the brickwork

On the street's far (bright) side ripple. Childhood's
     view.
My grandmother—an easy-to-see-through

Widow by the time she died—made it my own.
Bless her good sense. Far from those parts of town
Given to high finance, or the smash hit and steak
     house,
Macy's or crack, Saks or quick sex, this neighborhood
Saunters blandly forth, adjusting its clothing.
Things done in purple light before we met,
Uncultured things that twitched as on a slide
If thought about, fade like dreams. Two Upper
     East Side

Boys again! Rereading Sir Walter Scott
Or *Through the Looking Glass*, it's impossible not
To feel how adult life, with its storms and follies,
Is letting up, leaving me ten years old,
Trustful, inventive, once more good as gold
—And counting on this to help, should a new spasm
Wake the gray sleeper, or to improve his chances
When ceilings flush with unheard ambulances.

I AM A VICTIM OF TELEPHONE

When I lay down to sleep dream the Wishing Well
    it rings
"Have you a new play for the brokendown theater?"
When I write in my notebook poem it rings
"Buster Keaton is under the brooklyn bridge on
    Frankfurt and Pearl..."
When I unsheath my skin extend my cock toward
    someone's thighs fat or thin, boy or girl
Tingaling—"Please get him out of jail...the police are
    crashing down"
When I lift the soupspoon to my lips, the phone on the
    floor begins purring
"Hello it's me—I'm in the park two broads from Iowa...
    nowhere to sleep last night...hit 'em in the mouth"
When I muse at smoke crawling over the roof outside
    my street window
purifying Eternity with my eye observation of grey
    vaporous columns in the sky
ring ring "Hello this is Esquire be a dear and finish
    your political commitment manifesto"
When I listen to radio presidents roaring on the
    convention floor
the phone also chimes in "Rush up to Harlem with us
    and see the riots"

Always the telephone linked to all the hearts of the
     world beating at once
crying my husband's gone my boyfriend's busted
     forever my poetry was rejected
won't you come over for money and please won't you
     write me a piece of bullshit
How are you dear can you come to Easthampton we're
     all here bathing in the ocean we're all so lonely
and I lay back on my pallet contemplating $50 phone
     bill, broke, drowsy, anxious, my heart fearful of
     the fingers dialing, the deaths, the singing of
     telephone bells
ringing at dawn ringing all afternoon ringing up
     midnight ringing now forever.

MY SAD SELF
To Frank O'Hara

Sometimes when my eyes are red
I go up on top of the RCA Building
     and gaze at my world, Manhattan—
          my buildings, streets I've done feats in,
          lofts, beds, coldwater flats
—on Fifth Ave below which I also bear in mind,
     its ant cars, little yellow taxis, men
       walking the size of specks of wool—
Panorama of the bridges, sunrise over Brooklyn machine,
     sun go down over New Jersey where I was born
       & Paterson where I played with ants—
my later loves on 15th Street,
     my greater loves of Lower East Side,
       my once fabulous amours in the Bronx
               faraway—
paths crossing in these hidden streets,
     my history summed up, my absences
       and ecstasies in Harlem—
—sun shining down on all I own
     in one eyeblink to the horizon
       in my last eternity—
               matter is water.

Sad,
      I take the elevator and go
          down, pondering,
and walk on the pavements staring into all man's
                       plateglass, faces,
      questioning after who loves,
      and stop, bemused
          in front of an automobile shopwindow
      standing lost in calm thought,
          traffic moving up & down 5th Avenue blocks
                   behind me
          waiting for a moment when . . .

Time to go home & cook supper & listen to
          the romantic war news on the radio
               . . . all movement stops
& I walk in the timeless sadness of existence,
      tenderness flowing thru the buildings,
          my fingertips touching reality's face,
      my own face streaked with tears in the mirror
          of some window—at dusk—
                where I have no desire—
for bonbons—or to own the dresses or Japanese
      lampshades of intellection—

Confused by the spectacle around me,
    Man struggling up the street
        with packages, newspapers,
                ties, beautiful suits
      toward his desire
    Man, woman, streaming over the pavements
        red lights clocking hurried watches &
           movements at the curb—

And all these streets leading
    so crosswise, honking, lengthily,
        by avenues
    stalked by high buildings or crusted into slums
        thru such halting traffic
           screaming cars and engines
so painfully to this
    countryside, this graveyard
      this stillness
          on deathbed or mountain
   once seen
        never regained or desired
          in the mind to come
where all Manhattan that I've seen must disappear.

ST. VINCENT'S

Thinking of rain clouds that rose over the city
on the first of the year

in the same month
I consider that I have lived daily and with
eyes open and ears to hear
these years across from St. Vincent's Hospital
above whose roof those clouds rose

its bricks by day a French red under
cross facing south
blown-up neoclassic facades the tall
dark openings between columns at
the dawn of history
exploded into many windows
in a mortised face

inside it the ambulances have unloaded
after sirens' howling nearer through traffic on
Seventh Avenue long
ago I learned not to hear them
even when the sirens stop

they turn to back in
few passersby stay to look
and neither do I

at night two long blue
windows and one short one on the top floor
burn all night
many nights when most of the others are out
on what floor do they have
anything

I have seen the building drift moonlit through
        geraniums
late at night when trucks were few
moon just past the full
upper windows parts of the sky
as long as I looked
I watched it at Christmas and New Year
early in the morning I have seen the nurses ray out
        through
arterial streets
in the evening have noticed internes blocks away
on doorsteps one foot in the door

I have come upon the men in gloves taking out
the garbage at all hours
piling up mountains of
plastic bags white strata with green intermingled and
black
I have seen the pile
catch fire and studied the cloud

at the ends of the jets of the hoses
the fire engines as near as that
red beacons and
machine-throb heard by the whole body

I have noticed molded containers stacked outside
a delivery entrance on Twelfth Street
whether meals from a meal factory made up with those
mummified for long journeys by plane
or specimens for laboratory
examination sealed at the prescribed temperatures
either way closed delivery

and approached faces staring from above
crutches or tubular clamps
out for tentative walks
have paused for turtling wheelchairs
heard visitors talking in wind on each corner
while the lights changed and
hot dogs were handed over at the curb
in the middle of afternoon
mustard ketchup onions and relish
and police smelling of ether and laundry
were going back

and I have known them all less than the papers of
        our days

smoke rises from the chimneys do they have an
        incinerator
what for
how warm do they believe they have to maintain the air
in there
several of the windows appear
to be made of tin
but it may be the light reflected
I have imagined bees coming and going
on those sills though I have never seen them

who was St. Vincent

ROOM OF RETURN

Room over the Hudson
Where a naked light bulb
Lights coat hangers, whisky bottles,
Umbrellas, anti-war tracts, poems,
A potted plant trimmed to a crucifixion,

From which, out the front window,
You sometimes see
The *Vulcania* or the *France*
Or a fat *Queen*
Steaming through the buildings across the street,

To which every night
The alleycat sneaks up
To slop his saucer
Of fresh milk on the fire escape,
Washing down his rat,

Room crossed by winds from
Air conditioners' back ends,
By the clicking at all hours of invisible looms,
By cries of the night-market, hoofbeats, horns,
By bleats of boats lost on the Hudson,

Room, anyway,
Where I switch the light on
After an absence of years
Tiny glimmer again in this city
Pricking the sky, shelled by the dirty sea.

RUNNING ON SILK

A man in the black twill and gold braid of a pilot
and a woman with the virginal alertness
flight attendants had in the heyday
of stewardesses go running past
as if they have hopped off one plane
and run to hop on another.
They look to me absolutely like lovers;
in the verve and fleetness of their sprint
you can see them hastening toward each other
inside themselves. The man pulls a luggage
cart with one suitcase bungeed on top of another,
and the woman . . . my God, she holds her
high heels in her hand and runs on silk!
I see us, as if preserved in the amber
of forty-year-old Tennessee sour-mash whiskey
poured over cherishing ice, put down
our glasses, sidestep through groups
and pairs all gruffing and tinkling
to each other, slip out the door,
hoof and click down two flights of stairs.
Maybe he wonders what goes with his wife
and that unattached young man he left her
laughing with—and finds them not
where he left them, not in the kitchen,
not anywhere, and goes out to the hall and

hears laughter jangling in the stairwell
cut off by the bang of the outside door. In the street
she pulls off her shoes and runs on stocking feet
—laughing and crying *taxiii! taxiii!*
as if we were ecstatic worshipers springing
down a beach in Bora-Bora—toward a cab
suffusing its back end in red brake light.
As I push her in, a voice behind us calls
bop! bop! like a stun gun, or a pet name.
Out the taxi's rear window I glimpse him,
stopped dead, one foot on the sidewalk,
one in the gutter, a hand on his heart. *Go! go!*
we cry to the driver. After we come together,
to our surprise, for we are strangers,
my telephone also starts making a lot
of anxious, warbling, weeping-like noises.
I put it on the floor, with a pillow on it,
and we lie back and listen with satisfaction
to the rings as if they were dumdum bullets,
meant for us, spending their force in feathers.
A heavy man trotting by knocks my leg with his bag;
he doesn't even notice and trots on.
Could he be pursuing those two high-flyers
who have run out of sight? Will I find him, up ahead,
stopped at a just-shut departure gate, like that man
that night forty years ago, as if turned to wood
and put out by his murderers to sell cigars?

A SEDENTARY EXISTENCE

Sometimes you overhear them discussing it:
the truth—that thing I thought I was telling.
What could it have been that I said?
To be more or less like other men and women
and then to not be at all—it's

like writing a book that is both beautiful and
    disgusting.
Because we can't do it now. Yet this space
between me and what I had to say
is inspiring. There's a freshness
to the air; the crowds on Fifth Avenue
are pertinent, and the days up ahead,
still formless, unseen.

To be more or less unravelling
one's own kindness, noting
the look on others' faces, why
that's the ticket. It is all the expression
of today, and you know how we keep an eye on

today. It left on a speeding ship.

SO MANY LIVES

Sometimes I get radiant drunk when I think of and/or
     look at you,
Upstaged by our life, with me in it.
And other mornings too
Your care is like a city, with the uncomfortable parts
Evasive, and difficult to connect with the plan
That was, and the green diagonals of the rain kind of
Fudging to rapidly involve everything that stood out,
And doing so in an illegal way, but it doesn't matter,
It's rapture that counts, and what little
There is of it is seldom aboveboard,
That's its nature,
What we take our cue from.
It masquerades as worry, first, then as self-possession
In which I am numb, imagining I am this vision
Of ships stuck on the tarpaper of an urban main,
At night, coal stars glinting,
And you the ruby lights hung far above on pylons,
Seeming to own the night and the nearer reaches
Of a civilization we feel as ours,
The lining of our old doing.

I can walk away from you
Because I know I can always call, and in the end we will
Be irresolutely joined,

Laughing over this alphabet of connivance
That never goes on too long, because outside
My city there is wind, and burning straw and other
        things that don't coincide,
To which we'll be condemned, perhaps, some day.
Now our peace is in our assurance
And has that savor,
Its own blind deduction
Of whatever would become of us if
We were alone, to nurture on this shore some fable
To block out that other whose remote being
Becomes every day a little more sentient and more
        suavely realized.
I'll believe it when the police pay *you* off.
In the meantime there are so many things not to
        believe in
We can make a hobby of them, as long as we continue
        to uphold
The principle of private property.
So what if ours is planted with tin-can trees
It's better than a forest full of parked cars with the
        lights out,
Because the effort of staying back to side with someone
For whom number is everything
Will finally unplug the dark

And the black acacias stand out as symbols, lovers
Of what men will at last stop doing to each other
When we can be quiet, and start counting sheep to stay
    awake together.

ALL AFTERNOON

All afternoon the shadows have been building
A city of their own within the streets,
Carefully correcting the perspectives
With dark diagonals, and paring back
Sidewalks into catwalks, strips of bright
Companionways, as if it were a ship
This counter-city. But the leaning, black
Enjambements like ladders for assault
Scale the façades and tie them to the earth,
Confounding fire-escapes already meshed
In slatted ambiguities. You touch
The sliding shapes to find which place is which
And grime a finger with the ash of time
That blows through both, the shadow in the shade
And in the light, that scours each thoroughfare
To pit the walls, rise out of yard and stairwell
And tarnish the Chrysler's Aztec pinnacle.

GET UP

Morning wakens on time
in sub-freezing New York City.
I don't want to get out,
thinks the nested sparrow,
I don't want to get out
of my bed, says my son,
but out in Hudson Street
the trucks are grinding and honking
at United Parcel, and the voices
of loud speakers command us all.
The woman downstairs turns
on the TV and the smoke
of her first sweet joint rises
toward the infinite stopping
for the duration in my nostrils.
The taxpayers of hell are voting
today on the value of garbage,
the rivers are unfreezing
so that pure white swans may ride
upstream toward the secret source
of sweet waters, all the trains
are on time for the fun of it.
It is February of the year 1979
and my 52nd winter is turning
toward spring, toward cold rain

which gives way to warm rain
and beaten down grass. If I
were serious I would say I
take my stand on the edge
of the future tense and offer
my life, but in fact I stand
before a smudged bathroom mirror,
toothbrush in hand, and smile
at the puffed face smiling
back out of habit. Get up,
honey, I say, it could be a lot worse,
it could be a lot worse,
it could be happening to you.

209 CANAL

Not hell but a street, not
Death but a fruit-stand, not
Devils just hungry devils
Simply standing around the stoops, the stoops.

We find our way, wind up
The night, wound uppermost,
In four suits, a funny pack
From which to pick ourselves a card, any card:

Clubs for beating up, spades
For hard labor, diamonds
For buying up rough diamonds,
And hearts, face-up, face-down, for facing hearts.

Dummies in a rum game
We count the tricks that count
Waiting hours for the dim bar
Like a mouth to open wider After Hours.

AMONG THE MISSING

Know me? I am the ghost of Gansevoort Pier.
    Out of the Trucks, beside the garbage scow
    where rotten pilings form a sort of prow,
I loom, your practiced shadow, waiting here

for celebrants who cease to come my way,
    though mine were limbs as versatile as theirs
    and eyes as vagrant. Odd that no one cares
to ogle me now where I, as ever, lay

myself out, all my assets and then some,
    weather permitting. Is my voice so faint?
    Can't you hear me over the river's complaint?
Too dark to see me? Have you all become

ghosts? What earthly good is that? I want
    incarnate lovers hungry for my parts,
    longing hands and long-since lonely hearts!
It is your living bodies I must haunt,

and while the Hudson hauls its burdens past,
    having no hosts to welcome or repel
    disclosures of the kind I do so well,
I with the other ghosts am laid at last.

TEARS AT KORVETTE'S

Inevitably, in Fifth Avenue
The past comes up to strike me like a rake
Stepped on in innocence: before my eyes,
Stung by the brusque repeal of fifteen years,
My old friend-enemy Gerson appears
To me in perigee, orbiting near
My earth for the first time in many moons
At undiminished speed, looking the same
At forty as at twenty, full of blame
And waste and numinosity and flame.
But now, he indicates, the tide is caught
At full and harnessed to his errant art,
Filling, last summer, a bare gallery
In Boothbay with a lone epiphany,
A one-man manifestation, a late show.
Soon, maybe, Hirschl, Adler, Perls will cast
Their tender shadows in his way at last—
    "But come on in with me. I got to shop
For toys. My daughter's birthday." In Korvette's,
Talking impasto and Cézanne and reds,
Wearing a single paint spot of gamboge
For buttonhole on his blue blazer, badge
Of art in action, Gerson picks his toys—
Plush Mr. Rabbit (up to seven years),
A Dolly Tea Set and Miss Tiny Tears—

And pays with big bills scattered from his hand,
And leaves with bundles cumbering each arm,
And says goodbye with a sad flash of charm,
And leaves, a divorcé, for his hotel
And Nancy's birthday party, held among
Those canvases which were not for so long.

VISITING CHAOS

No matter how awful it is to be sitting in this
Terrible magazine office, and talking to this
Circular-saw-voiced West Side girl in a dirt-
Stiff Marimekko and lavender glasses, and this
Cake-bearded boy in short-rise Levi's, and hearing
The drip and rasp of their tones on the softening
Stone of my brain, and losing
The thread of their circular words, and looking
Out through their faces and soot on the window to
Winter in University Place, where a blue-
Faced man, made of rags and old newspapers, faces
A horrible grill, looking in at the food and the faces
It disappears into, and feeling,
Perhaps, for the first time in days, a hunger instead
Of a thirst; where two young girls in peacoats and hair
As long as your arm and snow-sanded sandals
Proceed to their hideout, a festering cold-water flat
Animated by roaches, where their lovers, loafing
    in wait
To warm and be warmed by brainless caresses,
Stake out a state
Of suspension; and where a black Cadillac 75
Stands by the curb to collect a collector of rents,
Its owner, the owner of numberless tenement flats;
And swivelling back

To the editorial pad
Of *Chaos*, a quarter-old quarterly of the arts,
And its brotherly, sisterly staff, told hardly apart
In their listlessly colorless sackcloth, their ash-colored
        skins,
Their resisterly sullenness, I suddenly think
That no matter how awful it is, it's better than it
Would be to be dead. But who can be sure about that?

UPPER BROADWAY

The leafbud straggles forth
toward the frigid light of the airshaft   this is faith
this pale extension of a day
when looking up   you know   something is changing
winter has turned   though the wind is colder
Three streets away   a roof collapses   onto people
who thought they still had time   Time out of mind

I have written so many words
wanting to live inside you
to be of use to you

Now I must write for myself   for this blind
woman scratching the pavement   with her wand of
        thought
this slippered crone   inching on icy streets
reaching into wire trashbaskets   pulling out
what was thrown away   and infinitely precious

I look at hands and see   they are still unfinished
I look at the vine and see the leafbud
inching towards life

I look at my face in the glass   and see
a halfborn woman

EASTSIDE INCIDENTS

Aside from ashcans & halljohns & pigeoncoops
there were the sad backyards
the hot July stoops
There were those mad Valenti kids who killed my cat
with an umbrella
There was Dirty Myra who screwed the Rabbi's son
in the cellar
And there was Vito & Tony & Robby & Rocco
I see them now
eating poisoned mushrooms and vomiting air
killing Mr. Bloom the storekeeper
and getting the chair
I see them now
but they aren't there

THE WHOLE MESS ... ALMOST

I ran up six flights of stairs
to my small furnished room
opened the window
and began throwing out
those things most important in life

First to go, Truth, squealing like a fink:
"Don't! I'll tell awful things about you!"
"Oh yeah? Well, I've nothing to hide ... OUT!"
Then went God, glowering & whimpering in
      amazement:
"It's not my fault! I'm not the cause of it all!" "OUT!"
Then Love, cooing bribes: "You'll never know
     impotency!
All the girls on *Vogue* covers, all yours!"
I pushed her fat ass out and screamed:
 "You always end up a bummer!"
I picked up Faith Hope Charity
all three clinging together:
"Without us you'll surely die!"
"With you I'm going nuts! Goodbye!"

Then Beauty ... ah, Beauty—
As I led her to the window
I told her: "You I loved best in life

... but you're a killer; Beauty kills!"
Not really meaning to drop her
I immediately ran downstairs
getting there just in time to catch her
"You saved me!" she cried
I put her down and told her: "Move on."

Went back up those six flights
went to the money
there was no money to throw out
The only thing left in the room was Death
hiding beneath the kitchen sink:
"I'm not real!" it cried
"I'm just a rumor spread by life..."
Laughing I threw it out, kitchen sink and all
and suddenly realized Humor
was all that was left—
All I could do with Humor was to say:
"Out the window with the window!"

THE BRIDGE

Good evening, here is the news.
Tonight, here in Manhattan, on a bridge,
a matter that began

two years ago between this man
and the woman next to him, is ending.
And that concludes the news for tonight,

except the old news of the river's fairy light,
and the bridge lit up
like the postcards, the cliché views,

except that they have nothing to grip the bridge with,
and across the river all the offices are on
for safety, they are like overtyped carbon

held up to light with the tears showing.
The heart that is girded iron melts. The iron
bridge is an empty party. A man is a feather.

There are too many lights on.
It's far too fanciful; that's all;
the iron rainbow to the bright water bending.

Neither is capable of going;
they stand like still beasts in a hunter's moon,
silent like beasts, but soon,

the woman
will sense in her eyes dawn's rain beginning,
and the man

feel in his muscles the river's startled flowing.

RETURN OF THE NATIVE

Harlem is vicious
modernism. BangClash.
Vicious the way its made.
Can you stand such beauty?
So violent and transforming.
The trees blink naked, being
so few. The women stare
and are in love with them
selves. The sky sits awake
over us. Screaming
at us. No rain.
Sun, hot cleaning sun
drives us under it.

The place, and place
meant of
black people. Their heavy Egypt.
(Weird word!) Their minds, mine,
the black hope mine. In Time.
We slide along in pain or too
happy. So much love
for us. All over, so much of
what we need. Can you sing
yourself, your life, your place
on the warm planet earth.
And look at the stones

the hearts, the gentle hum
of meaning. Each thing, life
we have, or love, is meant
for us in a world like this.
Where we may see ourselves
all the time. And suffer
in joy, that our lives
are so familiar.

NIGHT PIECE
(AFTER DICKENS)

A fine bright moon and thousands of stars!
It is a still night, a very still night
and the stillness is everywhere.

Not only is it a still night
on deserted roads and hilltops
where the dim, quilted countryside seems to doze
as it fans out into clumps of trees dark and unbending
against the sky, with the gray dust of moonlight upon
    them,

not only is it a still night
in backyards overgrown with weeds, and in woods,
and by tracks where the rat sleeps under the
        garnet-crusted rock,
and in the abandoned railroad station that reeks of
        mildew and urine,
and on the river where the oil slick rides the current
sparkling among islands and scattered weirs,

not only is it a still night
wherever the river winds through marshes and mud
        flats fouled
by bottles, tires, and rusty cans, and where it narrows

through the sloping acres of higher ground covered
    with plots
cleared and graded for building,

not only is it a still night
wherever the river flows, where houses cluster in small
    towns,
but farther down where more and more bridges are
    reflected in it,
where wharves, cranes, warehouses make it black and
    awful,
where it turns from those creaking shapes and mingles
    with the sea,

and not only is it a still night
at sea and on the pale glass of the beach
where the watcher stands upright in the mystery and
    motion of his life
and sees the silent ships move in from nowhere he has
    ever been,
crossing the path of light that he believes runs only
    to him,

but even in this stranger's wilderness of a city

it is a still night. Steeples and skyscrapers grow
more ethereal, rooftops crowded with towers and ducts
lose their ugliness under the shining of the urban moon;
street noises are fewer and are softened, and footsteps
on the sidewalks pass more quickly away.

In this place where the sound of traffic never ceases
and people move like a ghostly traffic from home to work
    and home,
and the poor in their tenements speak to their gods
and the rich do not hear them, every sound is merged,
this moonlight night, into a distant humming, as if
the city, finally, were singing itself to sleep.

TO MY DAUGHTER THE JUNKIE
ON A TRAIN

Children we have not borne
bedevil us by becoming
themselves
painfully sharp and unavoidable
like a needle in our flesh.

Coming home on the subway from a PTA meeting
of minds committed like murder
or suicide
to their own private struggle
a long-legged girl with a horse in her brain
slumps down beside me
begging to be ridden asleep
for the price of a midnight train
free from desire.
Little girl on the nod
if we are measured by the dreams we avoid
then you are the nightmare
of all sleeping mothers
rocking back and forth
the dead weight of your arms
locked about our necks
heavier than our habit
of looking for reasons.

My corrupt concern will not replace
what you once needed
but I am locked into my own addictions
and offer you my help, one eye
out
for my own station.
Roused and deprived
your costly dream explodes
into a terrible technicolored laughter
at my failure
up and down across the aisle
women avert their eyes
as the other mothers who became useless
curse our children who became junk.

A TRIP ON THE STATEN ISLAND FERRY

Dear Jonno
there are pigeons who nest
on the Staten Island Ferry
and raise their young
between the moving decks
and never touch
ashore.

Every voyage is a journey.

Cherish this city
left you by default
include it in your daydreams
there are still
secrets
in the streets
even I have not discovered
who knows
if the old men
who shine shoes on the Staten Island Ferry
carry their world
in a box slung across their shoulders
if they share their lunch
with birds
flying back and forth
upon an endless journey
if they ever find their way
back home.

AUDRE LORDE   159

WHITMAN IN BLACK

For my sins I live in the city of New York
Whitman's city lived in in Melville's senses, urban
    inferno
Where love can stay for only a minute
Then has to go, to get some work done
Here the detective and the small-time criminal are one
& tho the cases get solved the machine continues to run
Big Town will wear you down
But it's only here you can turn around 360 degrees
And everything is clear from here at the center
To every point along the circle of horizon
Here you can see for miles & miles & miles
Be born again daily, die nightly for a change of style
Hear clearly here; see with affection; bleakly cultivate
    compassion
Whitman's walk unchanged after its fashion

DUST—A SURVIVAL KIT 9/11–10/11 2001

9/25

Two weeks breathing the dead

each breath marking each
stunning absence

ourselves as coffin,
winding sheet, urn
worm

but oh, of what is God made?

10/2

We lived among blossoming words
until some of them exploded, like one
human exploding another

say *human* again
try to feel the word
on your lips

10/11

The dead have dispersed.
It has rained on them twice
they have drifted to sea
ascended in mist

Breathe them once again

and begin

TOWARD A CITY THAT SINGS

Into the topaz the crystalline signals
of Manhattan
the nightplane lowers my body
scintillate with longing to lie positive
beside
the electric waters of your flesh
and
I will never tell you the meaning of this poem:
Just say, "She wrote it and I recognize
the reference." Please
let it go at that. Although
it is all the willingness you lend
the world
as when you picked it up
the garbage scattering the cool
formalities of Madison Avenue
after midnight (where we walked
for miles as though we knew the woods
well enough to ignore the darkness)
although it is all the willingness you lend
the world
that makes me want
to clean up everything
in sight
(myself included)

for your possible
discovery

"IF YOU SAW A NEGRO LADY"

If you saw a Negro lady
sitting on a Tuesday
near the whirl-sludge doors of
Horn & Hardart on the main drag
of downtown Brooklyn

solitary and conspicuous as plain
and neat as walls impossible to
fresco and you watched her self-
conscious features shape about
a Horn & Hardart teaspoon
with a pucker from a cartoon

she would not understand
with spine as straight and solid
as her years of bending over floors
allowed

skin cleared of interest by a ruthless
soap   nails square and yellowclean
from metal files

sitting in a forty-year-old flush
of solitude and prickling
from the new white cotton blouse

concealing nothing she had ever noticed
even when she bathed and never
hummed a bathtub tune nor knew one

If you saw her square
above the dirty
mopped-on antiseptic floors
before the rag-wiped table tops

little finger   broad and stiff
in heavy emulation of a cockney
mannerism
would you turn her treat
into surprise
observing

happy birthday

LOVE: WRATH

He was very much the less attractive of the two:
    heavyset, part punk, part L. L. Bean,
both done ineptly; his look as brutal as the bully's who
    tormented you in second grade.
She was delicate and pretty; what she was suffering
    may have drawn her features finer.
As I went by, he'd just crossed his arms and said,
    "*You're* the one who's fucking us all up!"
He snarled it with a cruelty which made him look all
    the more a thug, and which astonished me,
that he would dare to speak to her like that, be so
    unafraid of losing her unlikely beauty ...
But still, I knew, love, what he was feeling: the
    hungering for reason, for fair play,
the lust for justice; all the higher systems "Go": the
    need, the fear, the awe, burned away.

From WAR
October, 2001

Fall's first freshness, strange: the seasons' ceaseless
    wheel,
starlings starting south, the annealed leaves ready to
    release,
yet still those columns of nothingness rise from their
    own ruins,

their twisted carcasses of steel and ash still fume, and
    still,
one by one, tacked up on walls by hopeful lovers,
    husbands, wives,
the absent faces wait, already tattering, fading, going
    out.

*These things that happen in the particle of time we have to
    be alive,*
*these violations which almost more than any altar, ark, or
    mosque*
embody sanctity by enacting so precisely sanctity's desecration.

These voices of bereavement asking of us what isn't to be given.
These suddenly smudged images of consonance and peace.
These fearful burdens to be borne: complicity, contrition, grief.

COUPLE AT CONEY ISLAND

It was early one Sunday morning,
So we put on our best rags
And went for a stroll along the boardwalk
Till we came to a kind of palace
With turrets and pennants flying.
It made me think of a wedding cake
In the window of a fancy bakery shop.

I was warm, so I took my jacket off
And put my arm round your waist
And drew you closer to me
While you leaned your head on my shoulder,
Anyone could see we'd made love
The night before and were still giddy on our feet.
We looked naked in our clothes

Staring at the red and white pennants
Whipped by the sea wind.
The rides and shooting galleries
With their ducks marching in line
Still boarded up and padlocked.
No one around yet to take our first dime.

FOR THE VERY SOUL OF ME

At the close of a sweltering night,
I found him at the entrance
Of a tower made of dark blue glass,
Crumpled on his side, naked,
Shielding his crotch with both hands,
His rags rolled up into a pillow.

The missing one, missed by no one,
Bruised and crusted with dirt,
As all the truly destitute are
Who make their bed on the bare pavement.
His mouth open as in death,
Or in memory of some debauchery.

The city at this hour tiptoe-quiet,
A lone yellow cab idling at the light,
The sleep-woozy driver taking a breath
Of the passing breeze,
Cool and smelling of the sea.

Insomnia and heat drove me out early,
Made me turn down one block
And not another, as if running
With a hot cinder in my eye,
And see him lying there unclothed,
One leg quivering now and then.

I thought, What if the cops find him?
So I looked up and down the avenue,
All the way to where the pyre
Of the sunrise had turned the sky red,
For something to cover him with.

THE ARGUMENT RESUMED;
OR, UP THROUGH TRIBECA

It may not be forever, but
The zing of beauty in the middle
Of the day—this little kid, for instance,
Heading home in his stroller,
Radiantly silly in a knitted snowsuit,
Or those windows of snazzy bowls
A few blocks back, all of solid wood
But gleaming as from a kiln
(Somebody should pay good money for that.
Ah, to be rich!)... The zing, I say,
An dich as we take our constitutional
Does add a luster when a luster is needed,
And if that luster fades as we proceed
Elsewhere, there's no call to be
Bereft. We are left with our store
Of memories: the scent, maybe, of a herbal rinse
Familiar from childhood. Or the sky may echo
The blue of a favorite tie. But "forever"?
Doesn't that tend to detract from the glory
Of the thing? Glory must burst
On us like fireworks. If the gleam
Or the sweetness isn't fleeting,
How shall it bear repeating?
How should we dare to eat another

Sundae of sunsets? See where a peach
Glows among other peaches in the fruitbowl.
Such and no other is the soul.

IN PRAISE OF NEW YORK

As we rise above it, row after row
Of lights reveal the incredible size
Of our loss. An ideal commonwealth
Would be no otherwise,
For we can no more legislate
Against the causes of unhappiness,
Such as death or impotence or times
When no one notices,
Than we can abolish the second law
Of thermodynamics, which states
That all energy, without exception, is wasted.
Still, under certain conditions
It is possible to move
To a slightly nicer
Neighborhood. Or if not,
Then at least there is usually someone
To talk to, or a library
That stays open till nine.
And any night you can see Times Square
Tremulous with its busloads
Of tourists who are seeing all of this
For the first and last time
Before they are flown
Back to the republic of Azerbaidzhan
On the shore of the Caspian,
Where for weeks they will dream of our faces
Drenched with an unbelievable light.

MAN LISTENING TO DISC

This is not bad—
ambling along 44th Street
with Sonny Rollins for company,
his music flowing through the soft calipers
of these earphones,

as if he were right beside me
on this clear day in March,
the pavement sparkling with sunlight,
pigeons fluttering off the curb,
nodding over a profusion of bread crumbs.

In fact, I would say
my delight at being suffused
with phrases from his saxophone—
some like honey, some like vinegar—
is surpassed only by my gratitude

to Tommy Potter for taking the time
to join us on this breezy afternoon
with his most unwieldy bass
and to the esteemed Arthur Taylor
who is somehow managing to navigate

this crowd with his cumbersome drums.
And I bow deeply to Thelonious Monk
for figuring out a way
to motorize—or whatever—his huge piano
so he could be with us today.

The music is loud yet so confidential
I cannot help feeling even more
like the center of the universe
than usual as I walk along to a rapid
little version of "The Way You Look Tonight,"

and all I can say to my fellow pedestrians,
to the woman in the white sweater,
the man in the tan raincoat and the heavy glasses,
who mistake themselves for the center of the
        universe—
all I can say is watch your step

because the five of us, instruments and all,
are about to angle over
to the south side of the street
and then, in our own tightly knit way,
turn the corner at Sixth Avenue.

And if any of you are curious
about where this aggregation,
this whole battery-powered crew,
is headed, let us just say
that the real center of the universe,

the only true point of view,
is full of the hope that he,
the hub of the cosmos
with his hair blown sideways,
will eventually make it all the way downtown.

WALKING THROUGH THE UPPER
EAST SIDE

All over the district, on leather couches
& brocade couches, on daybeds
& "professional divans," they are confessing.
The air is thick with it,
the ears of the analysts must be sticky.

Words fill the air above couches & hover there
hanging like smog. I imagine
impossible Steinberg scrolls,
unutterable sounds suspended in inked curlicues
while the Braque print & the innocuous Utrillo
look on look on look on.

My six analysts, for example—
the sly Czech who tucked his shoelaces
under the tongues of his shoes,
the mistress of social work with orange hair,
the famous old German who said:
"You sink, zerefore you are,"
the bouncy American who loved to talk dirty,
the bitchy widow of a famous theoretician,
& another—or was it two?—I have forgotten—
they rise like a Greek chorus in my dreams.
They reproach me for my messy life.
They do not offer to refund my money.

& the others—siblings for an hour or so—
ghosts whom I brushed in & out of the door.
Sometimes the couch was warm from their bodies.
Only our coats knew each other,
rubbing shoulders in the dark closet.

BOY OUT IN THE WORLD

Our son at ten does not believe in evil,
he judges by himself, he knows no man
would willingly hurt another. He believes in
force, axe against lance, one cross-bow
against two swords, he believes in measurement,
power, division, blood, but not
the malevolent heart, so when he walks home
at 3 o'clock, on West 97th,
down our block past the junkie hotels,
the light burden of his pack on his back
dark-red as some area deep in the body
that is never seen, and the man says to him Hey, kid,
he answers, he meets force with force,
his arms so thin the light comes through the edges,
        he says
Yeah? And the man asks him a question, so
eager he is for this boy to explain the world,
the man says You know what *cock* means?
Our son answers politely and keeps walking,
he feels sorry for a man so dumb he has to ask
                        question like that,
and he knows it wasn't a bad man,
or a dangerous one, just a regular man,
not dressed like a bum or talking like a wino,
and anyway this boy knows what's what, he can

look deep into his own heart
and tell you the nature of the human—kindness,
courtesy, force.

JUST A NEW YORK POEM

i wanted to take
your hand and run with you
together toward
ourselves down the street to your street
i wanted to laugh aloud
and skip the notes past
the marquee advertising "women
in love" past the record
shop with "The Spirit
In The Dark" past the smoke shop
past the park and no
parking today signs
past the people watching me in
my blue velvet and i don't remember
what you wore but only that i didn't want
anything to be wearing you
i wanted to give
myself to the cyclone that is
your arms
and let you in the eye of my hurricane and know
the calm before

and some fall evening
after the cocktails
and the very expensive and very bad

steak served with day-old baked potatoes
and the second cup of coffee taken
while listening to the rejected
violin player
maybe some fall evening
when the taxis have passed you by
and that light sort of rain
that occasionally falls
in new york begins
you'll take a thought
and laugh aloud
the notes carrying all the way over
to me and we'll run again
together
toward each other
yes?

THE NEW YORKERS

In front of the bank building
after six o'clock the gathering
of the bag people begins

In cold weather they huddle
around newspapers
when it is freezing they get
cardboard boxes

Someone said they are all rich eccentrics
Someone is   of course   crazy

The man and his buddy moved
to the truck port
in the adjoining building
most early evenings he visits
his neighbors awaiting
the return of his friend
from points unknown to me
they seem to be a spontaneous
combustion these night people
they evaporate during the light of day
only to emerge at evening glow
as if they had never been away

I am told there are people
who live underground
in the layer between the subways
and the pipes that run them
they have harnessed the steam
to heat their corner
and cook their food
though there is no electricity
making them effectively   moles

The twentieth century has seen
    two big wars and two small ones
    the automobile and the SST
    telephones and satellites in the sky
    man on the moon and spacecraft on Jupiter
How odd to also see the people
of New York City living
in the doorways of public buildings
as if this is an emerging nation
though of course it is

Look at the old woman
who sits on 57th Street and 8th Avenue
selling pencils
I don't know where she spends the night

she sits summer and winter
snow or rain humming
some white religious song
she must weigh over 250 pounds
the flesh on her legs has stretched
like a petite pair of stockings
onto a medium frame
beyond its ability to fit
there are tears and holes
of various purples in her legs
things and stuff ooze from them
drying and running again
there is never   though   a smell
she does not ask you to buy
a pencil nor will her eyes
condemn your health
it's easy really to walk by her
unlike the man in front
of Tiffany's she holds her pencils
near her knee
you take or not
depending upon your writing needs

He on the other hand is blind and walking
his german shepherd dog
his sign says THERE
BUT FOR THE GRACE OF GOD

GOES YOU and there is a long
explanation of his condition
It's rather easy for the Tiffany shopper
to see his condition
    he is Black

Uptown on 125th Street is an old blind Black woman
she is out only in good
        weather and clothes
her house is probably spotless
as southern ladies are wont to keep house
and her wig is always on straight
    You got something for me, she called
    What do you want, I asked
    What's yo name? I know yo family
    No, you don't, I said laughing   You don't know
        anything about me
    You that Eyetalian poet ain't you? I know yo voice.
        I seen you on television
I peered closely into her eyes
    You didn't see me or you'd know I'm black
    Let me feel yo hair   if you Black   Hold down yo head
I did and she did
    Got something for me, she laughed
    You felt my hair   that's good luck
    Good luck is money, chile   she said
    Good luck is money

THREE WEEKS AFTER

Gravity works long hours, tall buildings come to rest
across our shoulders, the sky is different, and the hands
    of clocks
    spin to make us older.

Children are playing again but more quietly, as if
they were children who still had to learn
    how to lose themselves in shouting.

On the street I stop to talk to friends.
I touch his leather elbow, the blue of her coat. I look
at his remarkable face. How deep her eyes have become.

THE WORLD TRADE CENTER
1993

I never liked the World Trade Center.
When it went up I talked it down
As did many other New Yorkers.
The twin towers were ugly monoliths
That lacked the details the ornament the character
Of the Empire State Building and especially
The Chrysler Building, everyone's favorite,
With its scalloped top, so noble.
The World Trade Center was an example of what
     was wrong
With American architecture,
And it stayed that way for twenty-five years
Until that Friday afternoon in February
When the bomb went off and the buildings became
A great symbol of America, like the Statue
Of Liberty at the end of Hitchcock's *Saboteur*.
My whole attitude toward the World Trade Center
Changed overnight. I began to like the way
It comes into view as you reach Sixth Avenue
From any side street, the way the tops
Of the towers dissolve into white skies
In the east when you cross the Hudson
Into the city across the George Washington Bridge.

DAVID LEHMAN

OCTOBER 11, 1998

Of cities I know New York
wins the paranoia award
the place you'd least like
to be stuck between floors
on a temperamental elevator
on 14th Street or ride on
the N train when the
conductor's face is missing
that must be why we like it
we who like to think we
thrive on risk on the other
hand the discrepancy
between the cold air
outside and the overheated
flat is without parallel and
completely without justification

SEPTEMBER 14, 2001

Before September 11
I would have written it
one way. I would have
interviewed the soldier
who volunteers to die
as penance for his part
in the erotic shipwreck.
He had understood her
as little as she had
understood him though
there were children
to consider and now
they were orphans.
I would have depicted
the plane crash as an
accident in a world of
disorder not a careful
calculation. But now
they love us, because
we've taken this hit,
and in case you forget
all you have to do is
look up and it's not there.

IN THE AGE OF POSTCAPITALISM

The disabled garment worker
who explains to his daughter
he's God the Holy Spirit
and lonely and doesn't care
if he lives or dies;
the secret sarcoma shaped like a flower
in the bowels of a pregnant woman;
ashes in the river, a floating chair,
long, white, shrieking cats;
the watch that tells Zurich,
Jerusalem and Peking time;
and the commodities broker
nervously smiling, mouth slightly twitching
when he says to the police he's forgotten
where he left his Mercedes:
everything attaches itself to me today.
Thirty million—the American
Broadcasting Corporation World News
conservatively estimates—
murders already this century.
Whether the public debt
may have affected case history
Number 51's excuse that she was abandoned
on the pier by a dolphin
and the question "What Has Become of

the Question of 'I' "
are topics for discussion
at the Institute for Political Economy.
I know all about the transmigration of souls.
I know about love and about strife.
To delight in a measured phrase,
to bank the rage in the gut,
to speak more softly,
to waken at three in the morning to think only of her
—in the age of postcapitalism.
Yellow and gray dusk thickens around the Bridge.
Rain begins to slant between
the chimneys and the power plant.
I don't feel like changing,
or waiting anymore either,
and I don't believe we're dreaming
this October sixth, in New York City,
during the nineteen eighties.

LOVE

He looks like a bowling pin, she looks like the ball.
All over the neighborhood, I meet them,
walking hand in hand, his stretching way down to hers.
They waddle walk as really fat, or stupid, people do.
When I climb the stairs and pass their apartment
I see them sitting at their kitchen table.
They always leave their door open at dinner time.
The smell of cabbage and old linoleum overpowers
     the hall.

His face is like a shy bell, fat and friendly at the bottom.
Her shape is shapeless with an overall impression
     of round.
He has a gray-flecked crew cut and an expression like
     a cow.
She has wispy mouse hair and cackles through rotten
     teeth.
I make small talk with them as they lumber up the stairs:
"You're out late," I say. "We're out late," he giggles.
"We're out late," she echoes. "It's late," he elaborates.
Poor, stupid, mismatched and ugly, they have love.

Yesterday, the Super told me that she was dead.
She had stepped out between parked cars and
got run over by a truck.

I walk up the stairs past their closed door
and picture him sitting on the padded chrome chair,
staring at the pearly formica of the kitchen table,
his big, shy hands hanging between his knees, unheld,
and I cry.

MAN ON A FIRE ESCAPE

He couldn't remember what propelled him
out of the bedroom window onto the fire escape
of his fifth-floor walkup on the river,

so that he could see, as if for the first time,
sunset settling down on the dazed cityscape
and tugboats pulling barges up the river.

There were barred windows glaring at him
from the other side of the street
while the sun deepened into a smoky flare

that scalded the clouds gold-vermilion.
It was just an ordinary autumn twilight—
the kind he had witnessed often before—

but then the day brightened almost unnaturally
into a rusting, burnished, purplish red haze
and everything burst into flame:

the factories pouring smoke into the sky,
the trees and shrubs, the shadows
of pedestrians singed and rushing home...

There were storefronts going blind and cars
burning on the parkway and steel girders
collapsing into the polluted waves.

EXPULSION

In the cab, light plays down his neck from behind
making the collar shine, making his lifted fingers describe
something inhuman
even though they only meant to indicate
emphasis or touch the
glass divider. Once
the light seems to let his whole hand come to
the very edge of the burning
field. She thinks he touched her with it once
but can't recall. Did he? Were they nearing
their address? Cloud-cover gathered. At the studio, John
showed them two different prints of the Bresson
in which a figure seen from behind is running up
—or is it into?—an incandescent village (Greece),
            walls gone,
difference gone, shine, shine,
and then three windows and the one black door
that cut the light
making it come
true—Oh it's a city. And there are stairs. And there's
a girl about to
disappear.
According to which print you see, she's running towards
            something
or desperately away.

When greys govern it looks like fate, what holds the
     white
place down—
(barely)—
In the high-contrast print it looks like history—
They say this to each other holding one print in either
hand,
and then the photograph of Moore a week before she
     died,
then Faulkner looking away, back to the snarling dogs.
I think we misunderstand the Hopi injunction
against the photograph.
It's not that it steals the soul away.
Rather that *being-seen* will activate that soul,
until the flesh is something that can be risen through,
until the face you offer up is the one that can't be
helped.
Give me that look that says you know I'm seeing you
     but you
don't care, John said, sit still, yes
that's the look now, yes, that's
beautiful.
What was it she wanted to tell him
about the light as they left,
light coming to do what can be done
to hold a city?
Brick, glass, she might have whispered,

it slips in gratitude off of the wires he would have
said,
they cannot hold it, it loves them best—
Reader,
now it's almost visible to them, the *after wards*,
the face of the god who wouldn't be seen except from
        behind,
hand on his piece of rock,
hand pressing down where the young man hides.
What can you find looking up from this white page
        now,
what can you find across the room? Or is it a store? An
avenue?—See how they glow even now these minutes,
        this hiding
place—
Lord what were they meant to have done with it
        (shine, shine)—?
To take it up entire into themselves? extinguish it?
sucking the whole field up into the
present tense, turning each thing again and again
in their hands as if to see it *from all sides at once*, that
dream—
the visible having stood still for them for over a thousand
years whispering *describe*, whispering *take me
back in*—?
Isn't that what place had wanted
them for?

OVERHEARD IN THE LOVE HOTEL

Again the cab slips west down 14th almost
To the river—
The cobbled meat market, steel grates down;
A thrown-up Christmas tree
Lot on an old dock beyond the stalled highway;
A whiff of blood and the first snow
That keeps not falling.

We've just checked into the Love Hotel—
Film noir signatures on the register:
"Tom Neal," "Ann Savage";
Spouses discarded, even her
Two other lovers forsaken at the bolted door.

Fading polyester roses drape the bed—matching
Trellis on an overhead mirror; evening breeze
Out of Hoboken through cracked panes
—Nothing can dispel the half-life traces of
        Roach Bomb
She chases with a blunt cigar . . .
"So sexy you brought these. This is sweet—
And throws a little curve into the day."

Blue ice pail; Absolut from a frosted cup.
Raking her new coil of brassy curls,

"Can you picture me with grey hair?
My mother passed her forties as a blonde;
Now you know my true color—

You and a few others."
Wrapping her ankles around his, she pins
Him on the spread
As from a room upstairs springs rattle to a finish;
"It's like I'm one of them . . .
All the passion, the ecstasy—
We spend the rest of our lives trying to shake."

Reflected along the ceiling, freckles
From her back rotate constellations
He traces like a blind man reading a star map;
"You've got to see who I am—
These yearnings, sometimes they last two years,

Or they can burn out after all of seven seconds;
But they're intense, and very real."
The wall phone rings—*Twenty minutes, please.*
"I wish I could say I didn't know
How they call just before your time's up,
Or not getting your hair wet in the shower,
The towels that irritate your skin"—

Six-inch scar across her panty-line
Where last spring the surgeon
Scooped out her insides,
Reddening with soap and steam;
And still stings when she wears silk.

Outside, snow holding. Another cab.
"Where was I, tonight? I've been
Lying to Kevin about Steve, Steve about Kevin;
And to Stanley about both of them . . .
Only you have the whole story.
First time I lie to you—
Then you'll know we're really going someplace."

CONSTRUCTION SITE, WINDY NIGHT

Great plastic sheets are flapping
twenty stories up, east and south,
where tinted windows will look out
over the park next summer,

and widows will draw their blinds,
and men gripping iced drinks talk
about money and death
while the moon slides between clouds;

and up another ten stories,
the foreman's corrugated shack
rattles, and the rats tip
a pail of rivets onto the floor

where cats will doze, and young
girls waltz, and lovers groan,
oblivious of wild parties above
and children howling below;

and even higher, on the roof,
a flock of pigeons lines the railing,
and they will remain as they are,
scanning the blotted trees

and mating and sleeping
and squinting at the odd visitor
who will venture up on a summer night
to be alone or to meet someone,

to escape an argument
or to connect with the cosmos,
to stare down from that windy perch
at his fellow-citizens

crossing streets and hailing cabs
and think how far away they are,
and how the things men construct
in their minds can materialize

suddenly, towering over them
and filling them with dread of heights.

Trucks are salting the streets.
The airports have closed.
In this long empty room the shadow
of a lemon tree flutters on the wall.
The last record played hours ago,
but the stereo's lights,
like rubies and emeralds,
continue to flicker.
The blanket on the bed is paper-thin,
the pillow is like stone.
I was dreaming of myself
in such a bed,
drawing a map that encompassed
all the cities I just passed through—
Paris Trieste Athens Ravenna—
except that it resembled a map
of the Amazonian jungle,
vast forests and countless tributaries
off a serpentine river.
Until I wake up, I feel certain
this map could have guided me around Europe,
or anywhere else I chose to go.
Meanwhile, through the frozen window,
an ocean liner, white as an iceberg,
is sailing down the Hudson
for the open sea.

NICHOLAS CHRISTOPHER   203

THE LAST HOURS OF LAÓDIKÊ,
SISTER OF HEKTOR
(a poem of September 11)

Cold missiles and a rain
of embers accompany the men
who slide like shadows into the city
faces mud-smeared
stones for teeth no eyes

who slit the throats of everyone
they encounter until breaking down
my door they drag me into the darkness
that floods the corridor
and lock me in an icy chamber

where a torch of thorns sputters
and a man more bone than flesh
is playing music old
as time itself on a flute
and a girl clutching her knees

burns with fever before I apply
a square of moonlight to her brow
before she whispers her name
my name
both of us falling now

the room falling too and the city
and no one to hear our cries
just the dead waiting in a bottomless canyon
and the sound relentless
of the gods grinding this world to dust

A MARRIED COUPLE DISCOVERS
IRRECONCILABLE DIFFERENCES

We are riding through the city one night,
under trees. Hawthorn hedges flower
along the park drives.

Sitting on the passenger side,
I cup my hand in the wind outside the car.
I hold my hand to my ear:

What were you saying?
My hand gets colder.
The side of my face

near the window doesn't feel real;
the other side is hot
in the face of reason.

I agree with you, wholly.
But the hand out there
curves around with the wind,

draws it in,
filled with tree breath.
I can hardly speak.

GLASS

At 8 P.M., each office window
Is a propped-up laboratory slide from the Mad
      Scientist's files.

Slide A reveals a janitor who studies the dark in a
      doorway,
Slide B a clutter of memos folded into hats, and there

An executive hopeful nearly lost in fluorescent
      smudge,
Who plods late into the evening, alone, for little pay—

It's Mr. X of the Department for Redundancy
      Department,
Another pheasant under glass for the gods.

Gray angels nibble on his window ledge— ornithology
      knocking
On the door of evolution—and as he reaches to pet
      them

His hand flattens instead on that first page of the
      intangible,
That portrait of physics buried in the transparent.

IN THE SOUTH BRONX

Afternoons I walked past broken signs and bright graffiti,
dayglo signatures scrawled across abandoned buildings,
to the store I worked in—my father's store—
where my tasks were simple because I was a child:
dusting, sweeping, arranging greeting cards on narrow
    silver shelving.

But what I liked was sneaking off into the stockroom,
    its secret
dampnesses and darkness, where I waited for each
    complex trespass
that might find me and hint at something different,
    something beyond
the custody of money; how it would lead me away from
    those rigid gleaming
aisles with their orderly objects—some useful, some
    alluring,

and the register up front full of green and silver.
I'd sit among the empty cardboard boxes, each stack
    of them
like a mild endangered city slightly swaying,
while I thought of the children's hands, small as
    my own,
made livid in the store's fluorescent lighting,

and the way they'd hold out their palms so I could
      count for them
the few coins they'd carried so carefully from him:
Is this enough? Is this? Enough for what their mother
had sent them for: a kitchen clock, a ladle.
And often it was not. I wanted

to turn my face away in shame, but stood and swept
and piled the dirt into a dustpan, swept some more, and
      watched
how the shelves seemed never to grow empty (magic
      shelves!)
as they filled with *things*, so many things,
from assembly lines and sweat shops I hardly could
      imagine.

Each night we'd leave that neighborhood, though we'd
      once lived there,
riding back in our car toward the suburbs, past
      crowded neon streets,
and then onto the expressway, until finally we'd glide
      past the river
that balanced bright strings of light on its surface,
as if there were no hidden waste in it, no washed-up
      shoes, no broken moorings.

LAURIE SHECK   209

THE SUBWAY PLATFORM

And then the gray concrete of the subway platform,
     that shore
   stripped of all premise of softness
or repose. I stood there, beneath the city's sequential
     grids
   and frameworks, its wrappings and unwrappings
like a robe sewn with birds that flew into seasons of light,
   a robe of gold
and then a robe of ash.

All around me were briefcases, cell phones, baseball caps,
   folded umbrellas forlorn and still glistening
with rain. Who owned them? Each face possessed a
     hiddenness.
     DO NOT STEP ACROSS THE YELLOW LINE; the Transit
       Authority
had painted this onto the platform's edge
   beyond which the rails

gleamed, treacherous, almost maniacal,
   yet somehow full of promise. Glittery, icy, undead.
Sharp as acid eating through a mask. I counted forward
   in my mind to the third rail, bristling with current,
hissing inside it like a promise or a wish; and the word
   forward as if inside it also,

as if there were always a forward, always somewhere else
    to go: station stops, exits, stairways opening out into
        the dusty
light; turnstiles and signs indicating this street
    or that. Appointments. Addresses. Numbers and letters
of apartments, and their floors. Where was it, that thing
        I'd felt
    inside me, tensed for flight
or capture, streaked with the notion of distance and
        desire?
    And the people all around me, how many hadn't

at some time or another curled up in their beds with the
        shades drawn,
    not knowing how to feel the forwardness, or any trace
of joy? Wing of sorrow, wing of grief,
    I could feel it brushing my cheek, gray bird
I lived with, always it was so quiet on its tether.
    Then the train was finally coming, its earthquaky
rumblings building through the tunnel, its focused light

like a small fury. Soon we would get on, would step into
    that body whose headlights obliterate the tunnel's dark
like chalk scrawling words onto a blackboard.
    I looked down at the hems of the many dresses all
        around me,

they were so bright! Why hadn't I noticed them before?
    Reds
    and oranges and blues, geometrical and floral
        patterns

swirling beneath the browns and grays of raincoats,
    so numerous, so soft: *threshold*, I thought, and *lullaby*,
        disclosure,
the train growing louder, the feet moving toward the
        yellow
    line, the hems billowing as the train pulled up,
how they swayed and furrowed and leapt
    as if a seamstress had loosed them like laughter from
        her hands—

THE AMATEUR TERRORIST

I made all the wrong moves. first
of all I
hung around after
the explosion. I
made mental notes on
how quickly the firemen
arrived, how many
engines they thought
this was worth. I
was flattered; a six
alarm blaze! I
guess I acted too smug.

then there was the
woman. she was
a street vendor, a
harmless working-class
stiff, I thought
until she blurted out:
    *"Didn't I see you hanging around
        the building before the blast?"* a
dozen heads turned, a few of which
were cops. I

ran. she
looked as if she'd blown
the building up. she
blushed like a tattler
surrounded in a
  school yard.

DREAD

I'm going to tell you something
It's a simple fact of life.
If you're a young man in East New York,
Here's a simple fact of life:
If they don't shoot you with a gun,
They'll cut you with a knife.

I'm standing at the grave
Of a just-buried friend,
Staring at the fresh mound
Of a just-buried friend.
Don't know how it got started,
Can't see where it'll end.

Looked for a glass of water
But they gave me turpentine
You can ask for a glass of water
All you'll get is turpentine
I don't know why this life
Is like askin' a brick for wine.

I've lost eight friends already,
Who'll make number nine?
Lord, buried eight friends already,
Who'll be number nine?

I'd love to make plans with you, Sugar,
But I don't believe we'll have the time.

I sleep with the bullet
That didn't have my name,
Say *good morning* to the bullet
That didn't have my name,
So when my number comes up, baby,
It'll be the one thing you can't blame.

OUT OF CHAOS

No wonder some prefer a narrow hall,
A single room where doubts die
Until possibility, that odd flower,
Returns its face.

The doors close and open every day.

The doors close and open every day
And every day we hurtle toward the city.

Today I saw the usual human disaster:
Head in her chest, legs pocked with pink wounds,
Fingers wrapped tight around a white handbag.

Then the subway doors opened and children
Piled in: the whole car filled with their high
Broken music.

At the next stop they all poured out;
The car was vacant, solemn, the air
Settled and clear—but she was still there.

Outside a lilac bush blows to the wind,

And everywhere one looks
A pre-Socratic flux

Streams down avenues
Of taxicabs and radios,
Mortality's parade crowned with neon and chrome—

As if we were beasts evolving toward a sentence
That breaks and disperses before we arrive
At the city we promised to build.

A WEREWOLF IN BROOKLYN

Still almost blind in his thinking eye,
the last of the moon, as it zeros in
on the preordained spot, to modify
his downside structures and curry his skin

with its lucent brush, so the dog flares up,
he only can grasp as a metaphor.
A lozenge dissolves in a silver cup
out of which such emptinesses pour

to prove for him the Buddhists right
who say that wolfpacks of nothingness stalk
the signature stinks and blood trails of man,

but that to race with them and let them bite
will do for him much better than
Ping-Pong, kind visitors, electroshock.

IMMEDIATE CITY

Tall and plural and parallel,
their buff, excited skins
of glass pressed to glass and steel
bronzed by the falling sun,
the city's figmentary buildings dream
that they are one with the One.
Ignoring the office workers
trapped inside their neural nets,
they orient their ecstasy
up past the circling jumbo jets.
Older than the rocks is she

across whom their shadows float.
A million rivers navigate
the necklace at her throat.
The light that falls and falls
shatters in her million prisms.
In one of her million cubicles,
a man tunes his inner mechanisms,
types an endless memorandum.
Time moves slowly, then not at all.
A boy and two girls are
trading secrets down the hall.

YOU WEREN'T CRAZY AND YOU
WEREN'T DEAD

Four neat sonnets ago we were twenty.
You weren't crazy and you weren't dead.
We still counted ourselves four girlfriends
who'd gone to Radcliffe from the Bronx.

Later, nervous elegies, those four boxy
sonnets, emerged from my stunned hand.
I didn't have the courage to write them to you,
but to your parents, survivors again.

Your name in the synagogue's blue glass window
panel always makes me cry, and in the film
over my eyes I collect square Polaroids
of Purim costumes, graduations, day camps,

the mean permutations of the cubic friendship:
who was whose best friend, who telling secrets
to whom, who prettiest, smartest, the showoff, the bore.
A story of small, sorry memories.

The year after you killed yourself
the rest of us took a four-bedroom apartment.
The fourth was always changing owners.
We mentioned your name from time to time.

Your brother named his baby girl after you.
He seemed to leave the names of those others lost
in the war in the war.
I try to find comfort in this birth, this life,

the odd fact of another child with this name.
And, astonished that we have grown up, become
     mothers
five times over among the three of us,
the old numbers jumbled somehow and you

somehow gone out, away, or stayed behind,
I find the image of another, still young
Emily toddling into warped rooms all wrong.
Who will forgive her for what you did?

FROM THE CITY IN WHICH I LOVE YOU

Morning comes to this city vacant of you.
Pages and windows flare, and you are not there.
Someone sweeps his portion of sidewalk,
wakens the drunk, slumped like laundry,
and you are gone.

You are not in the wind
which someone notes in the margins of a book.
You are gone out of the small fires in abandoned lots
where human figures huddle,
each aspiring to its own ghost.

Between brick walls, in a space no wider than my face,
a leafless sapling stands in mud.
In its branches, a nest of raw mouths
gaping and cheeping, scrawny fires that must eat.
My hunger for you is no less than theirs

THE OWL AND THE LIGHTNING
—Brooklyn, New York

No pets in the projects,
the lease said,
and the contraband salamanders
shriveled on my pillow overnight.
I remember a Siamese cat, surefooted
I was told, who slipped from a window ledge
and became a red bundle
bulging in the arms of a janitor.

This was the law on the night
the owl was arrested.
He landed on the top floor,
through the open window
of apartment 14-E across the hall,
a solemn white bird bending the curtain rod.
In the cackling glow of the television,
his head swiveled, his eyes black.
The cops were called, and threw a horse blanket
over the owl, a bundle kicking.

Soon after, lightning jabbed the building,
hit apartment 14-E, scattering bricks from the roof
like beads from a broken necklace.
The sky blasted white, detonation of thunder.

Ten years old at the window, I knew then that God
was not the man in my mother's holy magazines,
touching fingertips to dying foreheads
with the half-smile of an athlete signing autographs.
God must be an owl, electricity
coursing through the hollow bones,
a white wing brushing the building.

WOMAN POLICE OFFICER IN ELEVATOR

Not that I'd ever noticed
Either a taste or a distaste
For that supposedly arousing
Rebus of pain and desire, the uniformed woman,
Whether as Dietrich in epaulettes,
Or armored like Penthesileia, or in thigh boots
And cocked hat, straddling the Atlantic,
Fishing for campesinos
With live torpedoes,

But when the rattling, john-sized
Tenement elevator paused
Mid-fall to blink a female housing cop
Into its humid cranium, I felt her presence
Spooling through me like a Möbius strip,
Splicing her spilling curls, nightstick, the gun at
      her hip,
Chrome shield, the breast it emblazoned,
Seamlessly into the same
Restless continuum . . .

I caught—was it possible?—
The scent of some sweet-tinctured oil;
Troubling, alluring; and looked away
Then glanced back obliquely: had I imagined it,

That sudden scimitar-glint of danger,
Or had some forbidden impulse—longing, lust, anger—
Tumid inside me like a hidden
Semiautomatic
In a schoolkid's lunch pack,

Triggered the blue-lashed, tiny
Metal detector of her eye?
I backed against my corner, watching
The numerals slowly swallow their green gulp of light;
Interminable! And as we fell,
Our little locked cube of stale air seemed to bristle
With a strange menace ... I thought of harms;
My own and not my own,
Contemplated or done;

Betrayals, infidelities,
Coercions, seductions, lies,
Ready to confess them all, and more,
As if in her firm indifference she'd regressed me
Inward down some atavistic line
To the original essence, the masculine
Criminal salt; a frieze of victims
Paneled in my own skull
Like a lit cathedral hell ...

A shudder, and then stillness;
Avoidance of each other's eyes
As in some bedroom fiasco's wake,
The air too brimful with disclosure, till the door
Opened and we parted, the clamped rift
Between us widening like a continental drift
Of the sexes; she to the butcher, the breaker,
The ripper, the rapist,
I to my therapist.

ANTIBODY

I've heard that blood will always tell:
tell me then, antigen, declining white cell count
answer, who wouldn't die for beauty
if he could? Microbe of mine, you don't have me
in mind. (The man fan-dancing from 1978
hit me with a feather's edge across the face, ghost
of a kiss. It burned.) Men who have paid
their brilliant bodies for soul's desire, a night
or hour, fifteen minutes of skin brushed against
bright skin, burn down to smoke and cinders
shaken over backyard gardens, charred
bone bits sieved out over water. The flat earth
loves them even contaminated, turned over
for no one's spring. Iris and gentian
spring up like blue flames, discard those parts
more perishable: lips, penises, testicles,
a lick of semen on the tongue, and other things
in the vicinity of sex. Up and down the sidewalk
stroll local gods (see also: saunter, promenade,
parade of possibilities, virtues at play: Sunday
afternoons before tea dance, off-white
evenings kneeling at public urinals, consumed
by what confuses, consuming it
too). Time in its burn is any
life, those hours, afternoons, buildings

smudged with soot and city residues. Later
they take your blood, that tells secrets
it doesn't know, bodies can refuse
their being such, rushing into someone's
wish not to be. My babbling blood.
What's left of burning
burns as well: me down to blackened
glass, an offering in anthracite,
the darkest glitter smoldering underground
until it consumes the earth
which loves me anyway, I'm sure.

WORKED LATE ON A TUESDAY NIGHT

Again.
Midtown is blasted out and silent,
drained of the crowd and its doggy day.
I trample the scraps of deli lunches
some ate outdoors as they stared dumbly
or hooted at us career girls—the haggard
beauties, the vivid can-dos, open raincoats aflap
in the March wind as we crossed to and fro
in front of the Public Library.

Never thought you'd be one of them,
did you, little lady?
Little Miss Phi Beta Kappa,
with your closetful of pleated
skirts, twenty-nine till death do us
part! Don't you see?
The good schoolgirl turns thirty,
forty, singing the song of time management
all day long, lugging the briefcase

home. So at 10:00 P.M.
you're standing here
with your hand in the air,
cold but too stubborn to reach
into your pocket for a glove, cursing

the freezing rain as though it were
your difficulty. It's pathetic,
and nobody's fault but
your own. Now

the tears,
down into the collar.
Cabs, cabs, but none for hire.
I haven't had dinner; I'm not half
of what I meant to be.
Among other things, the mother
of three. Too tired, tonight,
to seduce the father.

I SAW YOU WALKING

I saw you walking through Newark Penn Station
in your shoes of white ash. At the corner
of my nervous glance your dazed passage
first forced me away, tracing the crescent
berth you'd give a drunk, a lurcher, nuzzling
all comers with ill will and his stench, but
not this one, not today: one shirt arm's sheared
clean from the shoulder, the whole bare limb
wet with muscle and shining dimly pink,
the other full-sheathed in cotton, Brooks Bros.
type, the cuff yet buttoned at the wrist, a
parody of careful dress, preparedness—
so you had not rolled up your sleeves yet this
morning when your suit jacket (here are
the pants, dark gray, with subtle stripe, as worn
by men like you on ordinary days)
and briefcase (you've none, reverse commuter
come from the pit with nothing to carry
but your life) were torn from you, as your life
was not. Your face itself seemed to be walking,
leading your body north, though the age
of the face, blank and ashen, passing forth
and away from me, was unclear, the sandy
crown of hair powdered white like your feet, but
underneath not yet gray—forty-seven?

forty-eight? the age of someone's father—
and I trembled for your luck, for your broad,
dusted back, half shirted, walking away;
I should have dropped to my knees to thank God
you were alive, o my God, in whom I don't believe.

LET ME SAY THIS

We are here now but soon
we will not be here.
There are pigeons asleep in the sunlight
on the roof of the station house in Greenlawn;
there is an elderly woman on a bench
looking up from a crossword puzzle.
And on the train a girl cuts the curls
on a doll and talks to it
with the whimsical authority
of a mother of the inanimate
or the invisible, the way the woman
I used to meet in the restroom
in Penn Station was always fussing
and baby talking into a carriage
that, except for a few cans
and some garbage, was empty.

123RD STREET RAP

A day on
123rd Street

goes a little
something like
this:

Automatic bullets bounce
off stoop steps

It's about time to pay
all my debts

Church bells bong for
drunken mourners

Baby men growing on
all the corners

Money that
ain't mine

Sun that
don't shine

Trees that
don't grow

Wind that
won't blow

Drug posses
ready to rumble

Ceilings starting
to crumble

Abuelas close
eyes and pray

While they watch
the children play

Not much I
can say

Except day turns
to night

And I can't tell what's
wrong from what's right

on 123rd Street

WILLIE PERDOMO   237

NEW YORK, NEW YORK

A second New York is being built
a little west of the old one.
Why another, no one asks,
just build it, and they do.

The city is still closed off
to all but the work crews
who claim it's a perfect mirror image.

Truthfully, each man works on the replica
of the apartment building he lived in,
adding new touches,
like cologne dispensers, rock gardens,
and doorknobs marked for the grand hotels.

Improvements here and there, done secretly
and off the books. None of the supervisors
notice or mind. Everyone's in a wonderful mood,
joking, taking walks through the still streets
that the single reporter allowed inside has described as

"unleavened with reminders of the old city's
        complicated past,
but giving off some blue perfume from the early years
        on earth."

The men grow to love the peaceful town.
It becomes more difficult to return home at night,

which sets the wives to worrying.
The yellow soups are cold, the sunsets quick.

The men take long breaks on the fire escapes,
waving across the quiet spaces to other workers
meditating on their perches.

Until one day . . .

The sky fills with charred clouds.
Toolbelts rattle in the rising wind.

Something is wrong.

A foreman stands in the avenue
pointing binoculars at a massive gray mark
moving towards us in the eastern sky.

Several voices, What, What is it?

Pigeons, he yells through the wind.

DAVID BERMAN   239

CITY-AS-SCHOOL

Day-trips
in Washington Sq
Park, dropping

out——STONED
ON SAMO. Two hits
of acid a day

& each night
his father Gerard
worrying. Searches

the weeks high
& low. Finds his son
deep in a dice

game with God.
Blood
shot. Drags Basquiat

like a cigarette
back to Bklyn
to his high school

in the city—
"Papa I'll be very very
famous one day"

delirious Basquiat
declares. Hard
headed, mama's boy,

spleenless—
on a double
dare from Al Diaz,

fills a box with Papa's
shaving cream,
at graduation giving

Principal a white face
full of menthol.
NO POINT

IN GOING BACK—smart
ass Basquiat empties
his locker, heads

for the big city
with Papa's cash
loan. GOOD PLACE

FOR A HANDOUT.
EASY MARK
SUCKER. SURVIVING

CHILD WITH SEED OF LIFE—
knows only how to move
forward like a shark

or an 8-track, going
out of style. For broke.
PLUSH SAFE HE THINK:

Only the good
die numb—Bird
& Billie & Jimi

& Jesus—
his heroes
crowned

like a tooth.
GOLD WOOD.
Basquiat begins

with hisself, writes
FAMOUS
NEGRO ATHLETES

on downtown walls,
spraying SAMO
across SoHo—

"royalty, heroism
& the streets"—
covering galleries

with AARON
& OLD TIN. ORIGIN
OF COTTON. NO

MUNDANE OPTIONS.

ADONIS ALL MALE REVUE,
NOVEMBER 24

The sign asserts itself as you haven't for months. Ancient,
a few bulbs gone, the strip lights tangle and shirr behind

the rainy window of your taxi, which waits for the signal;
women are running against the traffic. Already the day

has sharpened into a bright, sordid night, already you
    should
have been home for dinner at the glass-topped table,
    staring

down at your unbodied feet. You would give almost
    anything
you own to throw the cab door wide, pay the three-fifty

the posters prescribe, and sit down in the front row
of the Adonis All Male Revue. Perched on a chair near
    the stage,

Venus is pausing, too. She has hidden her hair, her eyes,
    beneath
a scarf patterned in anemone petals. There is a tattered
    question

phrased around her face, inquiring after all the anonymity
     on stage
that bears his name. Hard, now, to recall specific desire
     and its elision:

for weeks she has waited to catch a single feature beneath
     the lights,
nursed a single drink, and all the time a weird wind has
     been blowing

across forty-second street, riffling the garbage. Outside, a
     pair of swans
rustles and worries on their tether while the time on the
     meter ticks away.

RAIN

Yesterday was the last day of summer.
And it makes sense
you weren't with me

then. Or even
on this rainy afternoon—

you're teaching me to live
apart from you, which has reduced to

breakfast dishes crowding the nightstand,
the TV droning with some Julie Christie drama,
my black hair unwashed for a fifth day.

After all what's grief to someone
who never tires of longing
except a manner of existing
in the present, where nothing is derivative.

Strange. It's much easier now
to reconcile
the scene of when I first saw you—

crossing a city street on a busy September afternoon.
The one perfect moment, before language.

LIBERTY ISLAND

On the street the trees throw off their whiteness, petals
like the paper discs a hole-punch makes or confetti
poured over the head of the girl who gave the party
where we met.

It was winter, downtown the snow was dyed pink where
a red envelope had been dropped, forgotten. All the
     parked cars
were trapped in snow banks.

We sat with our drinks by the window, a swag of
     postcards clipped
to a string on the wall. You told me about the island,
     the remote house
where, to see the ocean over the trees, you would stand
on the pitched roof, hugging the crumbling chimney.

Outside, on the sidewalk, all the freezing people
     grimaced,
waiting for us to give up our table.

And then what? At the concert we watched pairs of
     players,
perfectly aligned, attuned, making their beautiful noise
     out of the air

we coughed and whispered into. And then? This
     morning

what is saved? The daylight. I wake to the steady song
     of a bird; no,
a truck backing up in the street.

In the park with its view of Liberty Island I sit by the
     freshly planted
bed, the bulb's results lolling—fluted flowers in a
     neat line
pale-yellow and white. Everyone stops to watch
     them nod

in the new spring air. Today the trees are dressed,
     filled with fronds,
the water is glass all around us.

ACKNOWLEDGMENTS

Thanks are due to the following copyright holders for their permission to reprint:

ASHBERY, JOHN: 'A Sedentary Existence' from *Hotel Lautréamont* by John Ashbery. Copyright © 1992 by John Ashbery. Reprinted by permission of Georges Borchardt, Inc. 'So Many Lives' from *A Wave* by John Ashbery. Copyright © 1981, 1982, 1983, 1984 by John Ashbery. Reprinted by permission of Georges Borchardt, Inc. AUDEN, W. H.: 'September 1, 1939' copyright 1940 & renewed 1968 by W. H. Auden. 'Refugee Blues' copyright 1940 & renewed 1968 by W. H. Auden. From *W. H. Auden: The Collected Poems* by W. H. Auden. Used by permission of Random House, Inc. BARAKA, AMIRI: 'Return of the Native' from *Transbluesency: Selected Poems*, Marsilio Publishers. Reprinted by permission of the publishers. BAUMEL, JUDITH: 'You Weren't Crazy and You Weren't Dead' from *Now*, copyright © 1995 by Judith Baumel. Reprinted by permission of Miami University Press. BELLOWS, NATHANIEL: 'Liberty Island' first appeared in *The Paris Review*, Summer 2002. Reprinted by permission of the author and publishers. BERMAN, DAVID: 'New York, New York' from *Actual Air*, copyright © 1999 by David Berman. Reprinted by permission of Open City Books. BERRIGAN, TED: 'Whitman in Black' from *Selected Poems*, 1994. Copyright © Alice Notley, executrix of the Estate of Ted Berrigan. BISHOP, ELIZABETH: 'Letter to N. Y.' and 'The Man-Moth' from *The Complete Poems 1927–1979* by Elizabeth Bishop. Copyright © 1979, 1983 by Alice Helen Methfessel. Reprinted by permission of Farrar, Straus and Giroux, LLC. CHRISTOPHER, NICHOLAS: 'Construction Site, Windy Night' from *A Short History of the Island of Butterflies*, Viking Penguin, 1986. Copyright © Nicholas Christopher. Reprinted by permission of the author. 'The Last Hour of Laódikê, Sister of Hektor' © 2002 Nicholas Christopher. Reprinted by permission of the author. '1972, #43' from *Atomic Field*, copyright © 2000 by Nicholas Christopher, reprinted by permission of Harcourt, Inc. CLAMPITT, AMY: 'Dancers Exercising'